EVOLUTION CAN SUCK IT

FONZI BROWNWOOD

Poor Boys Publishing
Dallas, Texas

Copyright © 2014 by Fonzi Brownwood.

All rights reserved. No part of this publication may be reproduced, distributed or transmitted in any form or by any means, including photocopying, recording, or other electronic or mechanical methods, without the prior written permission of the publisher, except in the case of brief quotations embodied in critical reviews and certain other noncommercial uses permitted by copyright law.

Poor Boy's Press
Dallas, Texas
PoorBoysPress.com

Cover design by Fonzi Brownwood.
Cover images by Jef Thompson
(www.karmadogs.com/jef)

Evolution Can Suck It / Fonzi Brownwood -- 1st ed.
ISBN-10 061598066X
ISBN-13 9780615980669

*Dedicated to YOU.
And also Charles Darwin, who invented a bunch of stupid theories about humans.
Fuck that guy.*

ACT ZERO

....

THINGS THAT HAPPEN WHEN EVOLUTION TELLS YOU "HELLO"

YOU SAY SOME THINGS ABOUT YOURSELF THAT NO ONE GIVES A FUCK ABOUT

1.

In October, 1972, your mom pushed you out.
You're almost certain you were a push out, not a cut out.
Definitely a push out.
You became a crawl around.
Then you morphed into a walk around boy.
Not a boy with wings, or horns, or claws, or an amazing ability to predict the future, or any other unusual characteristic that would make you the star freak at a circus.
Nope.
You became a normal, ordinary, average, generic boy.
Two arms, two legs, a head filled with stuff, and a ding dong.

Enough to prove, if challenged, that indeed, you are a human boy.

Your mom will tell you that your first career choice was garbage man.
She'll tell it to you indirectly, in story form, to anyone with functioning ears.
She'll tell them, "he used to ride on the side of the shopping cart, and when I'd stop, he'd hop off and pretend to dump trash into the cart."
"Oh, really," the person on the receiving end of the story might say.
Or, they might use words like, "that's adorable," or "wow, OK," or "isn't that nice."
She'll continue, "a lady asked him one time what he wanted to be. He told her, 'I want to be a trash man.'"
"Oh, that's so cute."
At the age of four, your whole life planned out.
You don't remember any of this.

When you were in kindergarten, you wrote a thing titled, "The Day I Was Eaten By A Shark."
It was a brief piece of fiction about, something, probably being eaten by a shark.

Evolution Can Suck It

You wrote it in crayon on one of those tablets they used to make that had the face of an Indian (Native American, not a person actually from India) on it.
It won a prize.
First place, blue ribbon.
You haven't won any prizes for writing since then.

At around 9 years of consciousness, you wanted to wear tight fitting leather pants and bracelets lined with silver spikes.
You wanted to have long stringy blonde hair and a bad ass attitude.
You wanted to be just like the popular rock stars of the time.
You would listen to cassette tapes in your room and pretend to play the instruments.
You'd sing along.
You'd listen to a song over and over again, memorizing every detail.
When you'd see your cousin, you'd listen to records in his room.
He had the cool stuff, the stuff your mom wouldn't let you listen to, but that his mom didn't give a shit about.
The two of you would fight over who got to use the drumsticks.

FONZI BROWNWOOD

They were your cousin's drumsticks, but he didn't always want to be the drummer.
Those were the only times you got to be the drummer, when he didn't want to.
He was older, bigger, and stronger.

You still like playing pretend rock star.
But the enthusiasm is gone.

You wanted drums (see above to refresh).
But your dad bought you a guitar.
You took guitar lessons from a guy in a music store.
He had long, stringy, fake blond hair.
The first song he tried to teach you to play was titled, "You Really Got Me Now."
It was the version played by a popular rock band at the time.
One of your favorites.
The guitar player guy in that band was (still is) considered one of the best ever.
You had never held a guitar before.
And this is the song he wants you to learn.
Barre chords, slides, odd rhythms, and things that even an accomplished player struggles with.
You tried.
You failed.

Evolution Can Suck It

You quit.

In your teen years, nothing of particular importance happened.
You went to school like a good walk around boy.
Got decent grades.
Didn't get into much trouble.
Blah, blah, blah, whatever.
Oh, but once, there was this senior guy who wanted to kill you because you almost ran over his sister.
She was standing in the middle of the street at night talking to someone in a car.
You saw the headlights of the car, but didn't see her until it was too late.
She squeezed up against the other car to keep from getting run over.
You remember the look of terror on her face.
The senior guy was drunk, angry, very short, and had a reputation as someone who wasn't to be fucked with.
He ran after you and kicked the side of your car.
You drove off.
The next day after school, he corned you in your car and tried to start a fight.
But you were scared of him, so you just cowered.

He screamed words at you like "fuck," and "you better," and "shit."
Your friend was in the passenger seat looking on.
He called you a pussy afterwards, because you acted like a little pussy coward boy.
The senior guy never bothered you again after that.

You played baseball.
You liked it, but your coach didn't like you.
He forced you to also play basketball and run track.
It was a really small school, and you were the tallest person.
He needed you, even though you hated basketball.
You hated rubbing your sweaty, half naked body against other half naked, sweaty, possibly fat guys.
Your coach got pissed at you because you skipped out on a basketball tournament.
You chose to go to some dumb college thing, or something just as stupid as a basketball tournament, instead.
He tried talking you out of it.
You shrugged your shoulders and walked off, the equivalent of spitting in his face.
He got mad.
He made you run extra "horses" in basketball practice for two weeks.
He benched you in baseball.

Evolution Can Suck It

He yelled at you extra when you fucked up in anything.
"Come on, molasses," he'd scream at you.
(Molasses was your unofficial nickname, dubbed by some douche senior guy who was hot shit at the time.)
Your coach knew you liked baseball and hated all the other sports.
This was his way of letting you know he was in control.
This was your initiation into the world of gatekeepers.
You quit all sports shortly after.

You went to college right after high school.
Not real college, community college.
The 13th grade.
You quit after two years and got a real job at a mega-box store.

You got married when you were 21.
One of the reasons you quit school.
Another reason was because you were tired of school.

You got divorced before you hit 22.

You came home one day and found another guy sitting on your couch.
Your soon to be ex-wife was in the kitchen.
At the time, you thought it was weird, but didn't analyze it any further.
You didn't care.
You remember that feeling well.
Sometimes people say they don't care, but they don't really mean it.
They say it to try and convince themselves they don't.
But in this moment, you truly didn't care.
There's peace in not giving a fuck.
You never inquired about his presence.
You said "hi," changed into softball clothes, and left.
You never saw him or your ex-wife again.

A few years later, you went back to college.
This time for real.
Up to this point, you had just been a meandering nobody.
You thought college was going to change that.
It did.
It turned you from a meandering nobody into a meandering somebody with a job title.

Evolution Can Suck It

If you were ever free from the grips of The System, college retightened them.

2.

Today, you're a generic boy living a generic life.
You have a sit down and stare and type into computers all day job.
Your title is "Computer Typer Typing Boy II," or something equally stupid and generic.
You spend all your time on THE hunt to arrange your life to be comfortable.
Or on a treadmill running towards treasure (vague).
Or in pursuit of everlasting happiness (doesn't exist).
Or practicing the perpetual orgasm (messy).
Or in pursuit of perfection, where all the pieces fit neatly in place without much effort or thought (fantasy).
All the illusory things you've been trained to seek without question.
You've become a wind up doll.
The masters spent years installing the gears and the mechanisms that make you work.
Then more years winding the gears into place.
Then more years teaching you how to follow The Rut.

Then they set you off in pursuit.
A hunt for, whatever, things that will make you complete (slash) happy (slash) meaningful.
The big, fucking, LIE.

You weren't taught how to derive pleasure from simply being.
You were taught to obtain, consume, repeat.
Without those elements, nothing has meaning.
And meaning is paramount, a necessity.
Job + home filled with stuff + wife/husband + babies = perpetual orgasm.
An explosion of joy you can blast into anyone's face.
Including your own.
Like drinking your own piss.
Piss flavored orgasm juice, fire hosed right into your waiting mouth.
This is happiness.
(Don't do drugs, don't break the law, don't be gay, don't deviate from the path, don't talk to strangers, don't be a victim of serial killers, terrorists, Ponzi schemers, or Jehovah's Witness, all the things that destroy happiness.)

Save some money.
Retire.

Evolution Can Suck It

Die.

Death is the pursuit.

You spend your life arranging everything to be in place for when it occurs.

You can't die until all the pieces are in place.

Until you've been drained of all the little molecules of stuff that make up you, as a living creature outside the food chain.

Until your muscles turn to dust.

Until your body is shriveled and dehydrated and shivering.

THEN you'll be granted the sweet release of death.

And The Progress Machine will scoop you up, clearing a path for your successor.

ACT ONE

....

THINGS THAT HAPPEN WHEN EVOLUTION KNOCKS YOU OFF THE WORN PATH

YOU LOSE YOUR HOUSE

1.

You get a letter in the mail.
It reads, "I can help you with your mortgage troubles, Marie."
It's handwritten on yellow legal paper.
It's addressed specifically to you.
It makes you feel special, a tingling sensation in your pants.
"Marie, you are my princess in shining armor," you think.
Purple unicorns circle your head, shitting joy dust into your open mouth while chanting, "you are saved."
"Whatever," you shoo them away.

You dismiss the letter and open the rest of the mail.
There's a formal collection letter from the mortgage people.

When you quit your job and stopped paying your mortgage, nasty things started happening.
Like this daily reminder from the friendly mortgage people.
Reminding you of your obligation, that you're their bitch.
Reminding you that you have an anchor chained to an anvil noosed around your neck.
The notes have become increasingly threatening.
You haven't made a payment in 3 months.
It's been about 6 months since your last full payment.
They only count the full payments, the ones that contain all the interest, and taxes, and insurance, and the other shit they stack on top of the regular amount.

The text in the collection letter is so formal, arranged so neatly, probably written by a robot with a mountain of impressive credentials.
It uses words like "responsibility," and "obligation," and "duty."
And threats like, "you have until," and "pay this amount," and "foreclosure."
Threats designed to induce guilt and shame.
Weapons The System is fond of.

Evolution Can Suck It

And it always ends with a courteous, "if you need help paying your loan, please call our service department."
How nice of them.

You tried calling that number once or twice.
You were greeted each time by an apathetic "sales representative" who read from some script in response to all your questions/excuses.
They probably deal with people just like you every day.
The result of the call is always the same.
There's nothing they can do to help you.
In other words, PAY YOUR FUCKING BILL YOU FUCKING WORTHLESS FUCK.
That phone number is a fucking scam, a trick to get you to call in so they can try and guilt and shame you in real time.
You rip up the collection letter and throw it in the trash.

You eye the folded up yellow note on the counter.
You pick it up again and examine it, looking for anomalies, something to indicate it's insincere.
Junk mail spammers have grown sophisticated, resorting to convincing tricks to get you to take some stupid action, like call them or send them an email.

In doing so, they take your phone number or email address and use it as a bucket to piss in.
The ink seems real, written by hand, not printed by some expensive corporate printer.
The paper looks torn from an actual legal pad.
Hand torn, not torn by some robot in a factory.
The envelope appears to have been licked by a human tongue.
Marie's tongue, mmmmmm.

"Who the fuck is Marie," you think.
Sounds fake, made up.
You imagine calling this fictional sounding person, inviting her over.
She comes over, and turns out, she is a he.
Then HE uses some device to brainwash you into getting into his shitty looking rape van.
Then you wake up days later at some remote fortress, naked, butt hole sore, surrounded by other naked people chanting to some human wearing a Viking helmet and a cog piece.
He's mumbling about aliens and cattle and human sacrifice.
Then you realize, he's talking about shoving YOU into a cow's rectum and catapulting the result into space.
So the aliens don't destroy Earth, or something.

Evolution Can Suck It

You toss the letter back on the counter.
Not in the trash.
You're not ready to dismiss it yet.
You decide to let it percolate in your head.
Just in case human sacrifice turns into an appealing route.

2.

Your plan was to quit your job and start a business.
The formula was supposed to go something like this: no job + loads of time to start a business = freedom and lots and lots of $$$$$$$.
So much $krilla (gangsta) you could wipe your ass with it.
You could stuff wads of hundreds in a hobo's rotting mouth.
You could go to strip clubs every night and make it rain.
You could buy all the love and sex and friendship you need.
But reality has a way of pissing on your head.
YOUR head especially.
You failed to realize what a lazy fuck you are.
You failed to recognize just how clueless you are.

That guy that wrote that book you read about only working four hours a week brainwashed you into thinking you don't need to work hard to make a shit ton of money.

You don't, when you already have a shit ton of money.

You were suckered in to a high tech, new age get rich quick scheme.

A real mind fuck.

The formula goes something like this: read my blog + buy my "how to escape your miserable existence by doing things like I do them" seminar/class/book = freedom and lots and lots of $$$$$$ (not for YOU, for THEM).

The secret to making millions is selling the secret to making millions.

Suckers lap that crap up.

YOU'RE the biggest sucker God has ever invented. You sit here, disgusting, at 12pm, slightly hung over, on a Tuesday, playing video games, leaking money like an old man's asshole, still holding firm to the belief that jobs are evil.

You get up to get a soda.
There's the yellow piece of paper, still on the counter, skull fucking you.

Evolution Can Suck It

You don't even know who Marie is and she's already strapped on a virtual dildo and prepared it for violent anal intrusion.
YOUR ANUS.
"Fuck all this," you think.
"Fuck all this" is your catchphrase.
It's different incarnations: "fuck this," "whatever," "fuck it," "fuck me, I don't care," "fuck off," "fuck you fuck face."
You like to say those phrases because maybe it will make you truly believe you don't care.
You use it to try to push the anxiety and fear aside.
You'd like to be fearless and believe in "fuck all this," but you can't.

The yellow piece of paper with Marie's phone number handwritten on it is stapled to your consciousness.
God wants you to call it.
The same God who said, "uh oh, shit, that's too much," when injecting you with the sucker genes.
You fear God is trying to pull a prank on you.
He wants to see Marie strap on that big fat dildo and ram it in and out of your ass.
You imagine He gets a kick out of stuff like that.

You pop open the can soda and return to your video game.
You've been playing a level over and over again trying to beat your high score.
You sit and play this game, this same level, over and over, for hours.
Trying to get better, trying to learn from your mistakes.
It's a handy distraction.
If only you could apply this same pattern to everything else in your life.
Try.
Fail.
Learn.
Try again.
Fail again.
Learn.
Try, fail, try, fail, fail, Fail, FAIL, FAILURE, FUCKING FAILURE, YOU FAT FUCKING FAILURE PIECE OF FUCKING SHIT FUCK.

No one's around to criticize you when you fail in the video game.
You think maybe this would be a good place to settle in.

Evolution Can Suck It

Right here, on this cushion, on this couch, sitting forever playing the same video game, over and over.

Maybe order a blow up doll to sit next to you for company.

One that doesn't talk or move or have opinions.

That way, you're the only one with knowledge of your failures.

The other humans going about their business have no clue.

The humans that have jobs, lives, motivation, ambition.

You'll die one day taking all this knowledge of video game failure with you.

If this had been a date or a business or something else in the real world, others would compile this evidence and deduce that YOU'RE A FUCKING LOSER.

But in the video game world, alone on your couch drinking a soda, smelling of moldy beer, sitting next to an expressionless blow up doll, you're the only one that knows.

And if you exercise what you're thinking about exercising, which is calling the number on the yellow piece of paper, someone else will have evidence of your financial failure.

But if you put it off a few more days, play several hundred more games, maybe you'll accidentally trip and fall into a diamond mine.

"Fuck all this," you mumble out loud to no one.

3.

You see her pull into your driveway in an ordinary looking car.
You were expecting something fancier, a little more luxurious.
It's a plain, several-years-old car with a faded gray paint job.
You watch her get out, and again, are surprised by her ordinary-ness.
You were expecting someone "slicker," in a power suit, with that hairdo that all the corporate looking women wear.
Fashion that says, "I'm a professional of the female variety," without saying, "I'm a sexual creature looking for a man to fuck me."
Suppression of natural desires is strongly encouraged during business hours.

She's alone.

Evolution Can Suck It

You've often wondered the risk someone takes by showing up to a stranger's home alone.
How does she know you aren't a psycho kidnapper who's spent the last 3 years planning her elaborate death.
Maybe you've been plotting this all along, as an alternate personality that you don't know about, and you intentionally quit your job and let your house go in order for this moment to occur.

She's wearing a boring, ordinary business lady outfit, with boring heels.
Probably bought at a big box bargain clothing retailer.
The kind of outfit that says, "I ain't broke, but I'm also not wealthy."
She has boring black hair, and looks to be a boring age.
She has the appearance of someone traveling right down the meaty middle, where the masses collect and merge into a mound of sameness.
The same mound you like to hang out in because it makes you feel "different" (you aren't).

She saunters up the driveway.

You can hear her heels clicking with each step, muted by the glass and stucco dividing the air between the two of you.
She takes a left (her left) at the sidewalk and struts up to your door.
The doorbell rings.
Even though you are standing two feet from the door, you wait to answer it.
You like to make people think you weren't psychopathically watching them, analyzing their every move, hoping to catch them doing something embarrassing.
Like picking their nose and eating it, or shoving their thumb in their butt and licking the butt juice off.
You wait a few more moments, peering through the peep hole.
She's standing there calmly, almost expressionless.
All very business like.
A little TOO professional for your tastes.

You consider for a second not answering.
But she sounded so sincere on the phone, like she could genuinely help.
You never got the impression she was a scammer.
Why would a scammer come to your home, risking the slight possibility you have split personalities,

and that one of those personalities is going to kill her.

You click the deadbolt lock open and twist the door handle.
No turning back now.
Once the inside air meets the outside air, all your failures will be spilled into the world for everyone to analyze, criticize, and laugh at.
As the seals on the door part, you can hear the wind whisper "fucking loooooooooseeeeeerrrrr."

"Hi, I'm Marie," she smiles and offers her boring hand for the ceremonious shake.
"Hi, come in."
She walks in and says, "wow, what's all this," in a manner that suggests sincere indifference.
Like the words accidentally slipped out of her mouth and now she has to listen to the stupid answer.

You had turned the extra living room into a makeshift recording studio.
All the bonus money you received from the job you quit went into furnishing this room with all sorts of expensive recording equipment.

Amplifiers, acoustic panels hanging from the walls and ceiling by chains, microphones, guitars, effects pedals, and all sorts of overpriced cables strewn about.
You had visions of becoming a rock star, one of your childhood fantasies.
But the guidance counselor at your high school recommended against pursuing a music career, for practicality purposes.
"It's easier to get a job as an engineer than a musician," she told you in some form or another.
She might as well have said, "don't be stupid, follow the well-worn rut, get a real job you fucking idiot."
Or, maybe the guidance counselor didn't say any of that.
Maybe it was the little voice in your head, trained to steer you back to "practicality."
Conditioning that makes you believe you're making choices independently.
But in fact, it's The System steering you into the rut carved by the millions who fell prey to its influence before you.
A slight dissuasion is all it takes to turn the fearful onto the path worn.
It's the smart path, the safe path, the path everyone ordinary takes.

Evolution Can Suck It

THE FUCKING RUT.
And now you wonder why you're ordinary.
You've been trying to escape this reality by filling your extra living room with all this gear.
Gear that Marie fakes being impressed with.
And for a fraction of a second, you realize the futility of your existence.

"Yeah, it's a bunch of recording gear that I never use," you respond.
"Oh, it looks cool," she says.
You raise your eyebrows and crack a forced sideways smile, as if to say "thanks," but in a defeated way.

"Can you show me around?"
"Sure."
You take her around the house, showing her the other living room, the kitchen, the three bedrooms, the garage, and the back yard.
The dimensions that create the illusion of an ideal, happy, perfect, ordinary, boring life.

She seems mildly interested, but not really.
She's seen it all before.
You muster as much enthusiasm as you can, knowing the magnificence of the house will soon wear

off and you'll be all that's left, standing naked in front of the jury with all your shortcomings in the spotlight.
You've worked so hard to fill up the empty spaces with impressive stuff.
And this big, gorgeous, Titanic like house is the crown jewel.
The achievement of your life so far has been accepting the burden of debt in exchange for the privilege of living in this middle class palace.
Sparsely furnished, empty, cold, lonely.

"So what's the situation," Marie asks.
You're standing opposite her at the kitchen island; bent over, resting your elbows on the fancy granite counter tops.
You think for a moment of treating her like the mortgage people, telling her the same sob story you told them to get sympathy.
Instead, you opt for the truth.
"I quit my job because I hated it, and I haven't made a payment in about 5 months," you say.
She shakes her head in the affirmative motion, like she heard what you said but didn't really listen.
"So here's what I do," she begins in a matter of fact way, "I help people avoid foreclosure. In your case,

since you're already in default, the best course of action is to do a short sale."
She pauses and waits for some kind of response from you.
"I don't know what that is," you say.
She explains what a short sale is.
You nod the entire time, only partially understanding what she's telling you.
"The bottom line is, you sell your house, if the mortgage people agree to it, and you save yourself from full blown foreclosure," she says.
You think, "that sounds really good."
She says, "and we can only do this if you DON'T make another payment."
"Hmmm," you grunt, holding back a smile, "sounds good, let's do it."
You blurt it out without even thinking about it.
"Fuck all this," you say to yourself, smiling inside your head.

You've got nothing to lose, nothing to gain, nowhere to go.
Your life is at a standstill, and everything around you is spiraling out of your grasp.
It'll all pile up below your floating corpse, catch fire, and terminate this facade of an existence.
Freedom is in losing everything.

Freedom is dying, and being born again, and erasing all the burdensome, mundane THINGS that hang around your neck dragging you to the bottom of the ocean.
Once there's no more life to squeeze out of you, once THE MONEY RUNS OUT, the vultures will fly away.
Your ashes will float in space for a while, the wind will dissipate them, and no one will ever know you existed in this state.
No one will care.
Freedom is disappearing.
Freedom is losing everything again, and again, and again.

"Just to be clear, be sure to NOT make any more payments, because just one payment could screw up the whole process," she says.
"Ok."

You've been living mortgage free for several months.
You've come to the conclusion that it's the way God intended for you to live.
It's the way God wants everyone to live.

Evolution Can Suck It

Living a few more months without the burden of paying for a structure to house your body seems like more of a good thing.
She says, "I'll take care of everything."
"Ok."

4.

Marie came through for you.
She found a buyer (SUCKER) for your house and negotiated the deal with the mortgage people.
What a nice, boring lady.
She is your hero.
A true hero, not one of those glorified, fake ones.
There'll be no parades in her honor.
Oprah doesn't know she exists.
No one will make a movie or write a book about her.
But her heroism, coming to your aid, helping you when you needed it most, is a true act of kindness, sacrifice, and generosity.
She is the savior of the American dream.
The savior of you.

As a result of her triumph over evil, you had to move out of your middle class palace, back into the fucking "real world."

Back into the struggle, where it costs money to exist.
The air costs money, the water costs money, the food, the land, the booze, they all need a fresh and constant influx of money.
When the money stops, it all stops.
And you'll wither and die.
The System doesn't give a shit about your life, or your ability to live.
It only cares about sucking the money out of your pocket.
Especially, YOUR FUCKING POCKET.
Because you've sinned against the law of man.
You turned your back on the established order of things.
Your sentence is a starving bank account, the race towards the bottom, playing the zero sum game against the Goliath.
When you've been drained completely, your shriveled up corpse will be tossed into the path of The Progress Machine.
It'll scoop you up and haul you off to the recycling center.
A new, fresh human will be ushered in to occupy the space you vacated.
And the whole process will be repeated.
The same mistakes.

Evolution Can Suck It

The same struggles.
The same void that needs filling.

Marie version 2, please save these souls.

YOU GO TO JAIL

1.

The details are fuzzy.
The policeman tells you to get out of the car, shining his flashlight in your face. You're staggering drunk, barely able to comprehend his simple commands.
Where staggering = blackout, shit faced, on the verge of passing out.
Later, the police report will inform you that the cop had to tell you to put your car in park before exiting.

You're on a "back" street that runs through a typical, boring, suburban neighborhood, in a city known for encouraging the excessive behavior you've engaged in.
These "back" roads are supposed to be the covert way of evading the police when you're driving drunk.

But those sneaky fucking cops put someone here to catch you.
Probably thinking that anyone driving down this road at this time of night is up to no good.
Fucking assholes.

You slide out of the car and do your best to not walk and talk like someone who is slobbering drunk.
You've been told on various occasions that this is something you are very good at.
And, oddly, you feel proud that you possess this skill.
But there's a point where it's ineffective, where no matter how hard you try to exercise this skill, you can't hide the dirty truth.

The cop guides you to the back of your car.
You lean on your trunk.
<something happens you can't recall>

The cop asks you to walk a straight line, heel to toe.
You begin.
You stumble.
You begin again.
You stumble.
Fail.

Evolution Can Suck It

<something happens you can't recall>

The cop asks you to follow his pen with your eyes without moving your head.
He moves the pen to the right.
"Don't move your head," he commands.
He moves the pen to the left.
You move your head again.
Fail.
<something happens you can't recall>

You're leaning on the trunk of your car again, knowing that you've failed all the tests.
The cops says, "take a deep breath and blow into this until I say stop."
Your mind churns for a few seconds.
You remember reading something somewhere or seeing a thing on TV at one time that said you don't have to submit to a test like this.
"No," you say, feeling confidently defiant, and completely defeated at the same time.
You wobble a little and do your best to maintain eye contact with the stupid cop.
"This is your last chance to NOT go to jail," he says.
You think that's a pretty good argument, so you submit and blow into the tube.

"Keep going...keep going...keep going," he says.
The life is leaving your body.
"Ok," he says.

The cop looks at the device.
Waiting.
Waiting.
You're staring at his blank, matter-of-fact face, wobbling slightly, on the verge of slipping into a coma.
The device beeps.
He looks at you and says, "turn around and put your hands behind your back."
FUCKING FAIL.

Your friend is sitting in the passenger seat.
He leans his head out the window, "do I have to stay," he asks.
The cop says, "no, you can go."
He gets out of your car and walks off into the night.
You watch him walking down the road, staring at him the entire time.
Leaning forward on your trunk, hands cuffed behind your back, thinking, "there goes my only hope, what the fuck."
Your friend abandons you.

Evolution Can Suck It

The world abandons you.
Everyone is turning their back on you.
<something happens you can't recall>

The cop who is arresting you for driving while
stone fucking cold drunk needs to call another cop
to come pick you up, because it would be weird to
ride on the back of a motorcycle.
Sunlight is starting to crack the horizon.
You're fighting the urge to lie down on the ground
and go to sleep.
You've been awake for over 24 hours.
You've spent about 11 of those hours filling your
body with poison in the name of celebration.
It was your friend's birthday.
The same friend that just abandoned you.

The other cop arrives in a regular cop car.
He gets out and greets the motorcycle cop.
They say some things you can't remember and
laugh like cops.
He walks over to you, grabs your right arm, just
above the elbow, and guides you to the back seat.
He helps you inside.
The seat is hard plastic, not a regular, cushioned
one like you've seen in the movies.

There is a thick steel grate separating the back seat from the front seat.
You slunk down into the seat and inhale the lingering shame of those who occupied this seat before you.

2.

You arrive at the police station.
Jail.
Still shamefully slumped in the back seat, still shackled, still drunk.
The cop gets out and walks around the car and starts talking with some other dumb cops, laughing.
They've all got the same cop uniform on, the same dumb cop mustache, the same dumb cop arrogance.
Clones of one another.
Their voices are muted, incomprehensible from inside the cop car.
You somehow make out the muted words, "see ya later."

The cop walks over to your door and opens it.
He helps you get out.
You can barely stand.
Exhaustion is fully kicked in.

Evolution Can Suck It

The cop walks you to the entrance of the police station.
He makes you take off your shoes and put on bright orange slippers.
The same kind mental patients wear in the asylums.
He helps you keep your balance while you take your shoes off and put the slippers on, unwilling to remove the cuffs even for a second.

He guides you to a little room where one fat cop is sitting.
Bright fluorescent light paints every corner.
You're told to go in and stand across from the desk the fat cop is sitting at.
All the cops are pretty fat, but this guy is way fatter.
Maybe that's the reason he's sitting here instead of out chasing the bad guys.

Outside of the room is an area where other perpetrators are sitting, in full shackles.
From inside the room, you look out at your fate.
Everyone is quiet; sitting slumped, with their head angled down.
The humiliation of being in jail sinks in.

The fat cop in the little room stands up and walks over to you.
His uniform has the appearance of being painted on, the material stretched to its maximum.
It looks uncomfortable.
The cop that brought you in here comes back in the room.
Together, they turn your body to face a scratched up white brick wall.
One of them removes one side of the cuffs, freeing your right arm, but leaving the other wrist cuffed.
They wrap a chain around your waist, and put another cuff back on your right wrist and fasten both to the chain.
Now you can't even move your hands up to scratch your nose.
Then they both get down on one knee and install cuffs with a long chain between them to your ankles.
"Alright, go sit down," the fat cop says.

You choose a chair that is the furthest distance from another person.
You sit down and slump your body to match the demeanor of everyone else.
<something happens you can't recall>

Evolution Can Suck It

3.

"Do you need to write down any numbers from your phone," a cop asks you.
He seems empathetic, friendlier than the rest.
You shake your head in the affirmative motion.
He hands you your phone.
You try to turn it on.
The battery is dead.
Another score for the machines in the who-is-slave-to-who game.
"Oh well," the stupid cop says with a mocking snicker.

The cop guides you to where a woman wearing a nurse outfit is sitting.
He tells you to sit down and asks, "will you submit to a blood test?"
"No," you say.
"You can either submit or we can take it by force," the cop says.
Why did he fucking ask.
You suspect they like pushing people to their limits.
They like goading people to overreact and resist.

They get off on the power.
They get off on using their batons and Tasers and guns and other suppression devices.
They like to jack off to the violent, abuse of power fantasies in the community shower room.

You offer your arm for the blood sample without resistance.
A small let down for the dumb cops for sure.
You're still in cuffs, so you have to stand up into a squatting position to get your arm to rest as intended on the armrest of the chair.
The nurse lady puts a surgical tube around your upper arm.
She waits a couple of seconds.
Then she sticks the needle in and steals your blood.

The nurse lady presses a cotton ball onto the wound and quickly wraps some surgical tape around it to hold it in place.
A cop grabs your unwounded arm and guides you to stand in front of a roll up screen.
Opposite is a camera on a tripod.
The cop gets behind the camera and positions it.
This is the mug shot.

Evolution Can Suck It

But you were expecting to get to hold the little board that you've seen in so many other mug shots.
But nothing.
He takes a photo without warning.
"Turn to your right."

He leads you to another room.
It looks like a waiting room, similar to the one you left, but with administrative looking working spaces lining the walls, filled with administrative looking cops dutifully going about their business.

The cop guides you to a machine.
It has a touch screen that the cop uses to put in information about you.
Name.
Date of birth.
Where you house your body and possessions.
The number you're catalogued under in The System.
Height.
Weight.
Eye color.
You wait patiently while he types it all in.
You have nowhere to go, nothing to do.

The cop grabs your right hand and puts it flat against a sheet of glass and says, "hold it here."
This cop is also fat, and breathes heavily through his mouth, like a grouper fish.
He presses a button and the machine whirs for a couple of seconds.
Then a single bar of light turns on and moves the length of the glass, underneath your hand.
He removes your right hand and grabs your left hand and presses it against the glass.
More heavy breathing right into your ear, like he's competing in a decathlon in the Olympics while trying to seduce you.
He presses the button again.
While the bar of light scans your hand, he says something like, "hey, did you see that poop fart," to another cop standing in the area.
Some kind of cop joke.
You don't laugh.
Only the cops think it's funny.

He tells you to stand there while he pushes some buttons with his fat fingers.
He's squinting into the screen, mouth open.
This machine owns him.
He is its slave.

Evolution Can Suck It

He stares into it like he's trying to find its soul, in a trance.
His fat belly is spilling over the waist of his pants. Every button and seam of his uniform screaming in pain.
You're just standing there, a bread crumb being swept into the dumpster, staring at this fat cop who is a servant of the machine.
Time seems to stand still.
You're just standing there, meditating under the rush of chemicals your body is releasing that signal it's time to get some fucking sleep.
The feeling transcends being tired, almost like you may never sleep again.
Or that somehow you'll be frozen in this position forever, standing here slumped over, chained to yourself, staring at a fat cop staring into a machine.
The Future Explorers will replay this event over and over, analyze every detail, debate the meaning feverishly, and come to no uncontroversial conclusions.
The cop (finally) breaks his embrace with the machine and guides you to a specific seat in the waiting area.
"Sit here and don't move," he tells you, out of breath.

"No laying down. No speaking," he struggles to say the words.
"No getting up without permission," his final command.

A person in an orange jumpsuit with a long black number scratched on the back mops the floor.
He pauses frequently, appearing to take pleasure in his activity, smiling at nothing in particular.
He's the only one smiling who's not wearing a cop costume.

Another cop from behind you calls your name and commands you to go to another bank teller like window at the back of the room.
This window is lowered, in a sitting position, with a stainless steel stool growing out of the floor.
You sit on it.
You're still a little drunk.
The stool greets your butt with an icy welcome.
It's intentionally cold in this room.
The cold keeps the bad guys, like you, docile, subservient, and obedient.
There's something about being cold that lowers the desire to be aggressive.
You read that somewhere.

Evolution Can Suck It

"Hello," a lady cop greets you.
You say nothing.
You're not sure you're even capable of speaking.
You're not even sure if you're alive or dead.
She hands you a piece of paper through an opening at the bottom of the cage she's sitting in.
"Your bail is $3000. Your charge is DUI..." and she mumbles some other stuff you can't remember.
Your panic response builds.
You need to have someone pay $3000 to get you out of here.
If not, you'll be stuck here forever.
You don't know anyone who will pay that much.
It doesn't cross your mind to ask this robot lady any questions.
The desperation for sleep corrodes any rational thinking.
Being partially drunk doesn't help either.
"Go sit back down," she tells you.

4.

A cop reading names off a clipboard says your name.
You get up and go stand in line behind a guy with long, greasy black hair.

FONZI BROWNWOOD

He's a good foot shorter than you, and smells like piss.
You feel like punching him in the face until your fist breaks, or his face caves in, or you run out of anger (slash) frustration.

The cop leads you down a hall.
Branching off from the hall are doors.
Doors that lead to rooms.
Rooms that are occupied by people.
People who look like they're about to be executed.
Some rooms with more people than others.
A few overflowing with people.
Defeat enters your consciousness.

The cop unlocks a door and slides it open.
It's a heavy door, with a thick, scratched up glass window.
A man approaches the cop.
He wants to know when his court date is.
The cop ignores his question and yells at him, "shut up and go sit down."
The man obliges, and slinks back into the room.
The cop turns to your group, looking straight into your eyes, and motions for you to enter.
He slams the door closed and walks away.

Evolution Can Suck It

Half the people in the room are sleeping.
The other half are staring at a TV, which is blaring some popular, syndicated out-of-run sitcom that isn't funny.
The volume is so loud the speakers are crackling and vibrating the plastic encasement.
A bald, fat man is sleeping facing the wall on the floor, under a wooden bench.
Some people are sitting on the bench above him.
Looks like he's in a jail with legs as the bars.
He's using a roll of toilet paper as a pillow.

The cell is freezing cold.
Colder than the waiting area.
You're sitting on the floor against the back wall, only a few feet from a feces covered toilet.
You're almost directly under the TV.
The sound of canned humor vibrates your bones.
You pull your arms into your shirt and lean your head against the wall.

5.

An older man is sitting on the toilet staring right at you.
He's pushing and grunting, looking right in your eyes.

FONZI BROWNWOOD

A loving embrace.
You can hear the turds splashing into the toilet water.
Your knee jerk response is to wrap both of your hands around his exposed neck and squeeze until he stops struggling.
You don't do that for these two reasons:
What if you get poop on your clothes that you might have to continue wearing for a while.
What if his penis accidentally slips into your mouth, and his balls rest across the bridge of your nose, then someone takes a picture.

A cop comes to the door and opens it.
He says a few names.
Those people leave.
A few minutes later, another cop comes to the door with more people.
He opens the door and crams them into the cell.
It's like a subway train at rush hour.
The moment between people leaving and new people coming is your treat.

You angle your body towards the back wall, to keep the others from sneaking a peek at your baby maker while you pee.

Evolution Can Suck It

Because God will baste you in shame if another human outside the act of baby making sees your ding dong.

You wonder what time it is.
You wonder when they're going to come take you away.
You have to take a shit.
No way you use that toilet, and open yourself up to attack.
Maybe someone might try to stab you while you're shitting.
You'll die on a toilet in jail, covered with shit and piss and blood.
Disgraceful.

There's a guy sitting on the bench telling some other guy the story of his arrest.
He ran from the cops.
He had drugs and a gun.
He threw them away while running.
The cops zapped him with one of those stun guns.
It must have worked.
He held up his shirt, displaying two bloody holes on his back as proof.
He laughs.
The other guy laughs.

No one else laughs.

The guy using the toilet paper as a pillow hasn't moved since you've been here.
He might be dead.
No one cares.
You don't care.
You're jealous because he's doing the one thing you want to be doing.
All you want is to be released so you can return to your life of comfort.
You're sitting on a dirty floor, leaned up against a hard brick wall, adjacent to a shit covered toilet, under a blaring TV, in a room filled with criminals, most of which are drunk, with your arms folded inside your shirt, shivering slightly, exhausted, worried you're never going to leave here alive, worried that no one knows you're here, and even if they do, they don't care.

6.

This is the moment you realize you're in jail for real.
Everything up to this moment has been a dream.
Not any more.

Evolution Can Suck It

Time to get into the prison mindset and learn some life saving prison survival skills.
Like how to shiv people.
And how to defend your butt hole from others who want to put their penis in it.
And how to use that same butt hole to smuggle drugs and other stuff.
You continue sitting on the floor, leaned up against the back wall, mentally preparing for this future.
You train your mind, going over scenario after scenario, working them out to successful conclusion.

A man comes in wearing a blue jumpsuit.
He approaches you with a tray.
You take it.
A piece of white bread, a small thing of milk like you used to get in kindergarten, a small scoop of some brown stuff, some green beans, and an unripe banana.
You eat the bread and the banana and the green beans.
You taste the brown stuff.
You've never tasted actual shit before, but you imagine this is what it might taste like.

You fantasize about killing everyone in this room.

In your head, the cops find you sitting atop a pile of dead bodies, sipping from the kindergarten milk carton.
You killed them all using karate and prison food trays.
The cops burst in and fall down, slipping on the blood pooled on the floor.

Another man wearing a similar blue outfit comes in with a mop and a spray bottle.
He sprays chemicals on the floor and on the toilet.
You breathe the toxic fumes in deep, hoping for release.
He mops, wipes the toilet a little, and then leaves.
The chemical smell remains.
You get used to it.
You're getting used to this whole jail thing, also.
If only you could get some privacy to take a shit.

7.

The TV is blasting into your ear holes.
It's a once popular sitcom about a super lovable guy who's married, improbably, to a super hot girl.
They have kids and live in a house with two stories.
They have friends who are also married.

Evolution Can Suck It

The main friend guy is married, again improbably, to a different super hot girl.
They sit around and talk about stupid shit.
The women set up jokes for the men.
Jokes like, the woman says, "hey, did you see Stan watched football the other day."
Then the man would go, "yeah, and he ate half the pizza from the box then farted into his cupped hands and tried to show it to me."
Then a laugh track plays.
Your cue that the joke is over and you should also laugh.
But you don't.

The cops have tantrum-proofed the cell.
Nothing is removable by human muscle alone.
So no ripping up something and smashing it into the glass or against someone else's face.
Mental projections of violence aren't nearly as satisfying.
And ramming your own head into the wall repeatedly doesn't seem productive either.
Maybe if you take your shirt off and use it to strangle this motherfucker snoring next to you.
No.
Sit and take it.

FONZI BROWNWOOD

You found a phone attached to the wall earlier.
You tried using it to call the friend that abandoned you, but you couldn't remember his number.
You've delegated the duty of remembering things, like phone numbers and other trivial stuff, to the machines that have made you their slave.
The phone didn't work anyway.
A sweet sounding, but stern female voice kept saying, "the party you are trying to reach refused charges."

A cop opens the door.
He reads some names off a clipboard.
He reads your name.
You feel relieved.
Finally, you're going home.
Wait.
The cop hands you a paper grocery sack.
It's folded up and has your name written on it in all capital letters.
The cop finishes reading the names, closes the door, and says, "follow me."

You're taken to a room that is like a locker room, but without showers or lockers.
The walls are covered in the same type of bad graffiti you saw in the drunk tank.

Evolution Can Suck It

They're like ancient cave paintings.

You're instructed to go to a counter where a female cop is sitting.
"What size," she asks you.
You have no idea.
"Size for what," you ask.
Pants, shirt.
You give her your size.
She disappears into a row where stacks of jail attire are stored.
There's an outfit that has been sitting on a shelf, waiting for you to arrive.
A uniform crafted years ago by some third world, adolescent sweatshop worker.
Who's now probably fighting in some army in some war, somewhere, over some dumb political thing.
Or making shoes for some big shoe corporation.
The cop returns and hands you a blue outfit.
"Put this on. Put your clothes in the sack and bring it back to me," she orders.

You go to an unoccupied corner, strip off your clothes, except your underwear, and put on the blue outfit.

The pants barely fit and the top is too big, but not terribly too big.
This ain't a fucking fashion show.
There's no one to impress.
No women that will reject you because you're wearing an ill fitting blue jumpsuit.
No jobs to get fired from because you're not following some stupid dress code.
No one to project your own judgments on about how people should/shouldn't dress.
You relish the anonymity, the freedom from yourself.

You stuff your regular clothes into the sack with your name on it and take it back to the cop.
The cop orders you to go stand outside the locker room area, against the wall, and wait for the others to finish baptizing themselves in the holy correctional system waters.
One of the cops is waiting outside.
He's talking to another cop; different than the one you arrived with.
They're talking about stupid cop things.
They use words like "sometimes," and "also," and "man," and "oh," and "cool," and "oh yeah."
Their words are like static background noise that fades in and out of audibility.

Evolution Can Suck It

They all have the same stupid cop mustache, like factory-assembled robots running the same software.
Software that creates this desire to have a perfectly manicured mustache.

8.

A cop tells you to pick a cot.
Each cot has a sack on it.
You're told the contents of the sack are your new personal belongings.
But not really.
Because if someone stabs you in the throat or you get released, you don't get to keep them.
You pick a cot angled just right to view the TV, which is turned off.
You're a glutton for punishment.

The cop points to where the bathroom is.
It has a door that closes.
A safe place to expose your private parts.

The cop also points to the showers.
He says you're free to take one if you like.
You fear the shower.
That's where the butt rape happens.

It happens in every movie that's about prison or has a prison scene.
A weak person is standing in the shower, soap in their hair, eyes closed, oblivious.
Then, the people who do the raping, who are always muscular giants with huge ding dongs, come walking in and grab the weaker person.
Ominous music plays in the background.
The others hold him down or against the wall, still soapy.
They take turns raping his butt hole to completion.
There's one movie in particular, where after they rape the poor guy, they take a huge hunting knife and ram it into his already destroyed butt hole.
That scene repeats in your mind.

You go through the sack of stuff on your cot.
It's filled with things considered "necessities."
Stuff like a plastic toothbrush, sheets for the cot, soap, toilet paper, and a comb.

Shit is stacked up in your colon, but someone just went into the bathroom.
You decide to go take a shower.
You gather your tiny bar of soap and toothbrush, and head to the shower area.

Evolution Can Suck It

A small twinge of fear overcomes you as you strip down to nakedness.
The showers are actually sort of nice.
Each shower is private, with a curtain and everything.
Your only moment of solace since you've been here.
You listen for ominous music.

After not having a knife shoved in your butt during the shower, you put your blue outfit back on and go back to your cot.
The bathroom is still occupied.
Door's closed.
The guy on the cot next to you starts talking at you.
Just out of the blue, like the two of you have been talking for hours.
No traditional prison greetings, like, "Hi, my name is Ted, what's yours," or "hey, what's you in for?"
Just a conversational ambush, "'dis my fif time hear. Turnt mysef in las nigh. Gots uh court dae in da mornin'"
You listen only because there's nothing else to do.
He tells you about his court date and how he "turnt" himself in.

You only half understand the lingo of the institutionalized.
The jest of the story is, this isn't his first time in jail.
This is his "fif" time through these glass walls for the same offense.
The same thing that has brought you to this intersection with him.
"Fuck him," you think.
You don't care about his dilemma.
He keeps talking.
You shake your head as if you're paying attention.
At this moment, you just want to go take a shit and avoid getting ass raped and/or beat up.
You just want to survive.

The person occupying the bathroom exits.
You immediately get up and hustle to beat anyone else who might be thinking about emptying his bowels.
"Fuck them," you think.
You get to the bathroom and close the door.
There's no lock.
Fuck.
Anyone could come bursting in here and strangle you.

Evolution Can Suck It

You'd die face down, ass exposed, covered in shit and piss and blood.
Disgraceful.
Regardless, you drop your pants and sit on the toilet.

9.

The lights come on and some weird noises blast from the PA speakers.
A stupid cop says, "meal time."
This will be your third meal.
Each one has been increasingly bad.
It's always a kindergarten serving of milk, with a piece of bread, some green beans, a pile of mushed up brown stuff, and an unripe banana.
Might as well be elephant shit.
You eat the banana and the green beans.
You taste the mushy brown pile.
ASS.
Like you just licked the inside of a camel's rectum right after it pooped.

The same guy that vultures what everyone else doesn't eat appears.
Other than these moments, when uneaten food is present, you'd have no idea he exists.

He spends the time between meals sleeping on his cot, pretending to be dead.
You give him your tray and he slinks off into his corner of the world.

Real jail people start coming out of their cells.
These are the ones that do the butt raping and the stabbing and all the other bad things you've learned from watching prison movies.
These are the hardened criminals, in here for life, or at least for a really long time.
Institutionalized.
They don't give a fuck.
They view you as weak, as someone they can take back to their cell and consummate an unofficial marriage with.
You tense up and use worry as a shield.

A real jail person is walking by the cots, making his way towards yours.
He's whispering something.
Maybe it's threats, like, "watch your butts" or "I'mma get you" or "when you in my cell, you sit down to pee."
He's saying none of those things.
"Call Rainbow Bail Bonds and ask for Mike," he repeats to everyone.

Evolution Can Suck It

"Who," you ask.
"Rainbow Bail Bonds, ask for Mike. Tell him Damon sent you and he'll hook you up. Hook you up, man."
He makes a fist and pumps it down, scrunches his eyebrows together, nods slightly, and bites his bottom lip while he says it.
He gives you the phone number and you repeat it inside your head so you don't forget.
"Damon is my friend," you convince yourself.

You dial the number.
The person on the other end accepts the charges.
"I need to be bailed out, Damon sent me," you tell the man on the other side of the phone, not knowing the proper etiquette or procedure for this sort of thing.
"What's you name," he asks.
You give him your name.
You hear some clicking and some heavy breathing. The real jail people are growing in numbers, and getting loud.
All you want to do is get the fuck out of here, no matter the cost.
"You're set to be released at 8am tomorrow morning," the guy on the other end of the phone says.
"Oh."

"I can bail you out, but you might as well wait."
You think for a second.
"Ok, thanks, I guess I'll wait it out."
Hope returns.

You don't know what time it is, but it's dark outside.
8am has to be close.
You lay down on your cot.
A cop uses his dumb voice over the PA, "meal time's over."
The real jail people make their way back to their cells.
The lights go out.
You stare at the ceiling.
The bottom is hard, and cold.

10.

The real jail people sound like they're about to start a riot.
Cops are patrolling by their cell doors, casually, not saying anything.
Likes it's part of the routine.
It's still dark outside.
The lights are still off.

Evolution Can Suck It

Someone is yelling, and you can't understand what he's saying.
Sounds like he's arguing with someone else.
The echoes distort his words.
You're exhausted.
You can't be sure if this is even real.
You hope for the riot to get started, so you can escape to sleep.

You wake up.
There are more people in the room.
A lot more.
All the cots are occupied.
Whereas before, only a quarter of the cots had persons claiming them.
Those sneaky cops must've smuggled these motherfuckers in here when you were asleep.
You get up and go get a gray tray with the same slop on it.
Kindergarten serving of milk, green beans, piece of white bread, unripe banana, and a small pile of brown stuff.
Oh, and a bonus, a cookie.
You eat the cookie, then the banana, then the green beans, then the bread.

You figure if you were a full time resident here, you'd lose roughly 10 pounds a week.
Until you became nothing.
One day, you'd wake up and be nothing but dust.
You'd still be conscious and aware and thinking, but you'd have no vessel to travel around in.
Not a ghost, but a person that no one knows exists.
All the bad qualities of invisibility.
They would think you escaped or something, and begin a massive manhunt for the volatile drunk driver on the loose in the city.
You'd instantly be placed at the number one spot on the most wanted list.
The news would run exaggerated stories about you possibly going around getting drunk and intentionally driving dangerously on sidewalks.
They'd say things like, "a drunken man escaped from jail today and is now drunk and on the loose in your neighborhood. Diane."
The camera would cut to a suspiciously attractive woman (like, she's pretty, but something is just not right about her).
She's wearing way too much makeup.
"That's right Tom, and we've had reports of him driving on the sidewalk targeting mothers walking their newborn babies in strollers."

Evolution Can Suck It

You think all male newscasters should be named "Tom."
And all female newscasters should be named "Diane."
The news would run with this story for a few days, until a new story is invented that they can sensationalize.
Through all this, you'd be stuck in a cell without a body.
Just an invisible presence, consciously aware of everything.
The cops would stick a fat guy with lots of tattoos in the cell.
Your replacement.
He would do nothing but lay around naked, jack off, and shove things in his butt.
And he would smell like a donkey covered in rhino piss.
And you could see and smell and hear everything, because you're trapped.
The rest of eternity would be spent in this state.
Until the reign of humans ends.
Then the reign of the apes comes without you knowing about it.
Then it ends.
Then something else becomes the dominant species.

Then an asteroid kills all life on Earth.
Then billions of years pass, until The Future Explorers arrive to find their salvation.
And you're left in the same spot, the same spec in the galaxy, looking at infinite space, unable to die or go to sleep.

11.

You're watching the TV.
Not really paying attention, just pointing your eyes at it.
It's a show about a married guy who has no spine, no balls, and is basically a male shell filled with soft, squishy cream.
You can relate.

It's bright outside now.
Nothing has happened since the last meal.
Jail is like that, nothing really happens.
It's an infinite holding pattern.

Everyone is asleep.
You wonder how they can sleep so soundly.
The thought makes you jealous.
You want to sharpen the end of your toothbrush and stab each one of them once in the neck.

Evolution Can Suck It

Just once.
So in the future, they'll be unable to sleep as if they're safe.

You see a cop approaching, holding a clipboard.
He comes into the room and starts reading names.
Your name is the third one.
He says, "pack your things in the bag they came in and leave it on your cot."
You stuff your prison belongings into the sack.
You pause for a moment and soak in the memories.
You're going to miss this cot.
It had become your home, your safe place.
A person approaches you, "hey man, can I take that cot?"
He says it in a soft voice, almost whispering.
You shake your head in the affirmative motion, not knowing if you have the authority to make such an assignment.

The cop reading the names orders you to get in a single file line.
You remember from elementary school, then high school, then college, then real life, how to get in a single file line.
Most of your life feels like it's been spent in one form of single file line or another.

Sometimes it's the metaphorical kind, like when people are talking and you get in the socially acceptable form of communication line to say your words when they're done saying theirs.
Sometimes it's the real, physical kind, like waiting in line to buy a thing at the store.
This is the prison kind, which feels similar to the elementary and high school kind.

You get in an elevator and go down.
No one talks.
Everyone is defeated, completely docile and accepting of whatever fate waits when the elevator doors open.
Will there be a devil waiting to plunge burning pitchforks into you.
Will there be a gang of hillbillies waiting to rape you.
Will the doors open to a bottomless chasm you'll be pushed into.

The doors open.
None of those things is reality.
It's just another hallway.

The cop leads you back to the room where you changed into the blue jumpsuit.

Evolution Can Suck It

There's a guy in the room talking about how he got caught.
He has black stringy hair and looks like he might still be drunk.
He says things like, "uh, you know," and "totally," and "yeah, man."
When he's not talking, he sits with his mouth open.
You can hear the words he's saying, but can't make sense of them.

You wind through another maze of hallways.
Even if you were to try and escape, you'd get lost.
You get in a different elevator and go down some more.
More hallways.
You come to a section that looks like the inside of a bank.
There's a long line.
A cop tells you to wait in line.
He goes up to the front and starts talking with a group of other cops.
They laugh and taunt the people in the line.
Saying stupid cop things, like, "I bet you never want to come back here again."
All the cops laugh.

Another cop says something like, "you wanna stay a few more days."
They can laugh and say whatever they want, because they have the guns.
You just stand there and stare at them.
Anger molecules enter your bloodstream, but your body is too tired to recruit the muscles necessary to exercise the rage.
And you're too scared of being shot or beaten with one of those black sticks and thrown back into hell.
So you stand there, with everyone else, and take it.

12.

The lady hands you a card with some numbers and other information printed on it.
She tells you to exit through another hallway, out the double doors.
You read what's on the card.
It tells you where your car is.
It tells you when your court date is.
It tells you other stuff that depresses you.
Seems like you've spent a lot of your working life trying to get to a point where you possess more money than is necessary to exist.

Evolution Can Suck It

Then you do something dumb, and The System pounces, stripping you of any hope to achieve such an unachievable goal.
Fines, fees, court costs, bail, taxes, it all piles up and conspires against your desires and dreams.
This IS the American Dream (Fallacy).
A constant ramming in the ass by the entities designed to keep you safe and comfortable.
Entities that provide anything but those two things.
But at least you're not suffocating in a pit with men wearing gas masks pouring gasoline in your mouth.
At least you're not having your intestines torn out manually by a sadistic midget who tricked you into the back of a van by wearing clown makeup and promising "a good time."
At least you're free to go, at this moment.
Cast back into the real world to begin the struggle over again.
The cycle of modern life.

It's early morning in a town known for encouraging the type of behavior that has landed you in this very spot.
You're in an alleyway, surrounded by garbage and broken dreams and crushed hopes.
You contemplate how you're going to get your car.

Your phone is still dead.
You have no money.
A few blocks away is a famous street where people gamble millions of dollars every day.
Establishments known for projecting the illusion of "striking it rich" inhabit every centimeter of real estate along the street.
"It" being a very, very, exclusively vague term.

You reach a building and go in.
The whirring and clicking sounds and the stale stench of cigarette smoke slap you in the face.
Your delirium from lack of sleep is coming to a head, spilling over into the anonymity this place offers.
The only true thing of value this place can offer.
Anonymity is an actual lifestyle here.
Single serving friends of the night.
Single serving girlfriends
Single serving happiness.
All washed clean by the time your eyes crack open the next day.

You go to the bathroom and sit on the toilet and enjoy the solace.

Evolution Can Suck It

You walk out of the bathroom, go to a store and purchase a fizzy beverage and empty calories in bar form.
You walk outside and get into a taxicab.
You tell the driver the directions to the location of your car.
He says it's on the other side of town, 45 minutes away.
"Whatever, can you take me," you ask.
"Yes."
You start the cycle again.

ACT TWO

....

THINGS THAT HAPPEN WHEN EVOLUTION PUTS YOU IN A PLACE CALLED "THE PIT"

YOU GET BRAINWASHED

1.

You're facing a dark computer monitor.
It reflects your aging face.
You feel defeated.
Just last week, you were basking in the freedom of funemployment.
But you lacked the nipple of comfort to feed from.
Now here you sit.
Captive.
Claustrophobic.
In a tiny room, packed shoulder to shoulder with others fighting for same leftovers.

A still image of a popular racecar driver is projected onto the wall at the front of the room.
It's the official mascot of the company.
You think she looks like a man.
While you wait for this "training" (brainwashing) to begin, you imagine her using her large penis to steer the racecar.

She raises her eyebrows arrogantly at the other drivers as she passes them, with her hands intertwined behind her head.
As if to say, "hey, look at me, huh, pretty cool, huh," in a stereotypical French accent.
Then she bends the tip of her penis into her mouth and dates herself during a pit stop.

The automated drones giving this "training" (brainwashing) said something important during your penis driving fantasy.
They started without asking you if it was OK.
Now they expect you to answer questions about the information they just said.
Information you totally didn't pay attention to.
One day, paying attention will be a thing of the past, and information will just be rammed into everyone's mind.
Whether they want it or not.
Kids will no longer have to go through the torture and grand expense of "college" (brainwashing).
They'll be able to get all the knowledge they need to function as cogs in the machine digitally injected into their blood cells.
And it'll all be labeled "organic."
An organic injection of knowledge.

Evolution Can Suck It

But for now, you have to pay attention, like paying a toll, only way more expensive.
Or paying a nervous, sweaty man in an alley to have sex with one of his Herpes-infested hookers.

You failed to pay the toll of attention.
So now you have to guess at the answers to the stupid questions.
On your first day, already a test of your ability to take orders.
And you're failing.

You answer with antagonistic questions of your own.
Such as, "oh yeah, what's it to you."
And, "I think this room needs more alligators. What do you think."
You didn't think they were going to collect the papers and read the answers.
But they do.
And now, you sit silently staring into the dark computer screen in front of you, like a prisoner on death row about to be executed.
You've never been terminated on day one.
You've quit on day one, but never given the ax.
You mind switches to worry and panic mode.
All because you don't have enough attention to pay.

You can't afford it.
Instead, you tried to pay with a women driving with her penis fantasy, which isn't an acceptable form of currency here.
You sit, waiting to be executed.

You see the "training" (brainwashing) lady pick up your piece of paper.
She looks at it for a second, and then scrunches her nose, like she just saw something disgusting.
She puts it down on the pile of papers of people who actually tried.
She picks up the next one.
You release your tension.

You find a glossy photo of the female car driver's face.
You start decorating it.
It came in a folder your new masters gave you.
Everyone has the exact same folder, because you're all the exact same person.
The photo of the female car driver was snuggled in with other papers that had a lot of words and blank spaces on them.
It's like an autograph card, with an image of her dressed in her car driver uniform.

Evolution Can Suck It

Her hair is floating off her shoulders slightly, like a gust of wind lifted it into that position, at just the right time, as the photographer snapped the picture.
Her face is perfectly symmetrical, blemish free, and the ideal level of tan expected of a girl who has her picture taken a lot.

You draw a pointy mustache and goatee on her face.
You add angled down eyebrows and mutton chop sideburns.
Now she looks like a pissed off, smiling musketeer (laud the contradiction).
This image will sit in your cubicle prison for the duration of your stay here.
You'll look at it every day.
Others who see it will comment on it.
They'll say things like, "I see you made some adjustments to <censored>'s appearance."
And, "that's an interesting look for <censored>."
You'll grunt something like, "yeah," or "uh huh," in response, authentically taking no interest in their conversation attempts.

The "training" (brainwashing) continues.
You missed another section.

Something about what this place makes and who buys it.
Your mind translates the information you totally didn't pay attention to, to: "blah blah blah makes worthless shit and sells it to ignorant moron suckers."
You'll come to discover this isn't far from the truth.

2.

The folder where you found the glossy picture of the girl you decorated has your name printed on it, in black, capital letters.
The letters stand out on top of a blurry background image.
The image looks like emotionless, human shaped apparitions sitting in a large room, arranged in a maze of cubicles.
You put your index finger on one of the faceless apparitions and say to yourself, "that's me."
There's an image of a smiling woman standing with her arms folded that fills the upper left half of the folder.
You smear your thumb across her printed lips and name her "Susan."
Because she looks like a Susan, or a Diane, or something equally ordinary.

Evolution Can Suck It

She's the perfect corporate metaphor.
Appropriately dressed, not too sexy, not too stuffy.
Smiling using just the right amount of mouth, no teeth showing.
Her arms are folded in a standoffish way, like she might be a whip cracker, but a friendly, approachable one.
One you wouldn't mind taking a beating from.
You think briefly of cutting a hole in the folder where her mouth is to use in the bathroom later when you get bored.

The automated drones order you to open the folder and pull out the first piece of paper from the right pocket.
You comply.
"Fill this out and we'll collect it later," the drone says.
There are words on the paper mixed with a bunch of blank lines.
Words like, "Name:_____."
And, "Date:_____."
And other more personally revealing blank lines to write information in.
Information you have to dig from your littered mind.

Stuff like, the important number assigned to you by The System at birth, your address, phone number, grandmother's maiden name, name of your first pet, who to tell in case you die or have something tragic happen to you while working in your cubicle prison, etc.

The last blank line is, "Signature:_____."

When you make your mark on this blank line, you'll be expected to do the work.

HOLY SHIT THE FUCKING WORK.

If you knew right now what you'll come to know later, you'd set the building on fire.

You'd put on dark sunglasses, a leather jacket, inject yourself with steroids, go to the gym for years and get ripped, turn yourself into a robot, then travel back in time, to this moment.

You'd walk into the building, look around, and say, "I'll be back."

Then you'd drive a semi loaded with explosives into the building, ending this whole "training" (brainwashing) nonsense.

But you're ignorant right now.

You need the scraps they're trying to feed you.

The scraps they've dragged through fields of shit.

Scraps that the desperate people occupying this room are happy to receive.

Evolution Can Suck It

You sign your name in the blank space.

3.

You're told to pull out a little cardboard placard from the glossy folder.
"Please write your name so we know who you are," the drone says in a forced friendly manner.
You write the word "Superstar" on your placard, and draw a little pentagram as the punctuation.
This is the name you've dubbed yourself.
You are a superstar.
Like LeBron James, Kobe Bryant, Roger Staubach, Michael Jackson, Erkel.
Only no one else acknowledges your claim.
The others stare at your placard, grinning internally, probably thinking, "what an asshole."
You are an asshole, a diseased one, oozing blood and puss.
You proudly place the placard on the location of the desk designated for it, facing forward, so the drones can summon you when required without having to use their memory to produce your name.

The short, balding guy sitting next to you writes "Dave" on his.
"Conformist," you automatically think.

Then you realize you're in the same conforming boat as him.

You both voluntarily boarded it, implicitly agreeing that indeed, you are both following the rules one is supposed to follow.

You're the fucking conformist.

But somehow you're slightly different.

You're a "rebel."

You contemplate the term "rebel."

You defy authority by not writing your God-through-the-proxy-of-your-parents given name on a placard.

You defy authority by not paying enough attention.

You defy authority by drawing humorous facial hair on photos of female celebrity racecar drivers.

Fucking. Rebel.

You look up the definition of rebel: a person who resists any authority, control, or tradition.

"Yeah, bitch, that's me," you think.

You slink into your chair hoping no one challenges your conviction.

Because you know you're not really a rebel.

If you were, you wouldn't be sitting here, in "training" (brainwashing), filling out the papers necessary to enslave you, taking orders from automatons who stand at the front of the rooms and talk.

Evolution Can Suck It

A guy walks in.
He's short and bald, and looks important.
Like his name appears in a box higher than most other people in the chart that dictates who rules whom.
And above his name in that box is printed an authoritative sounding title.
Something like, "Sir Master Sir," or, "Lord Governor Highness," or, "Vice President."
You think "Vice" is bad ass, like an undercover cop who has authority to kill whoever he wants, and hot girls just drop to their knees and suck his dick when he's around.
You think about changing your title to "VICE Superstar."
Then you could go around stabbing other co-slaves in the throat whenever you felt like it.
Just having the word "VICE" in your job title gives you the authority to do whatever you want.
Stuff like, fuck girls in the men's bathroom with the door open.
Or punch people in the face for no reason.
Or kick your new "Lord Master Highness" in the nuts repeatedly.
Or command others to hold someone down while you shit in their mouth.
Being a "Vice Whatever" is cool.

The man that just walked in starts talking.
He's nervously looking around.
He introduced himself, but you misplaced (again)
the wallet that contains the attention.
He asks everyone to introduce themselves, then
points at a person sitting in the front row.
You're sitting as far back as a person can sit in this
room and still be considered in the room.
You calculate how long it will take to get to you, so
you can stop paying the attention toll for a while.
You need to conserve all the attention you can.
You calculate you have a few minutes.
So you stare into the darkness of the digital box,
but can't drift off into fantasy land.
You're too nervous.
"What am I going to say," you think.
Your blood pressure rises; you feel tingles, maybe
even a little sweat in your armpits.
You remember you wrote "Superstar" on your
placard.
And this little dwarf of an important man is using
the illusion of reading names to make this interaction appear personal.
Like he cares or something.
But you know he doesn't really care, because if he
could make a couple more pennies by firing every-

one in this room, he'd do it without a second thought.

"Superstar," he reads, with a fake smile on his face.
The others giggle a little.
Most of them had no clue you had rebelled against the establishment, defying authority by being a smart ass and writing "Superstar" on your placard, instead of your straight-from-the-Christian-bible given name, like all of them had done.
"That's right," you say, "it's my nickname."
"LIAR," your brain screams at you in fear.
"Hmmm," he replies.
He rocks back, folds his arms, and suspiciously asks, "so what makes YOU a SUPER star."
You dart your eyes towards the ground, "uhhhhhhh, uhhhh, because I'm the best."
"Is that so," he says, and winks, then unfolds his arms and moves on to the next person, "Dave."

Ugh, you made it through.
You fooled everyone.
They believe you're normal, albeit a bit quirky, but non-threatening.
People generally fear and despise a rebel, especially the people who are the target of the rebel's actions.
No one fears you.

FONZI BROWNWOOD

You're docile, obedient, conforming.
You fucking conformist.

You sit and stare into the dark box, wondering how all this is going to turn out.
Wondering if you made a mistake.
Wondering what all this means.
It means nothing.
Absolutely nothing.
You are now back on the grid, re-integrated with The System.
You are safe here, a member of the collective (again).
The warm blanket of extreme comfort wraps around you.

YOU DEVELOP AN ANXIETY DISORDER

1.

You've dug a trench to follow.
A trench to replace conscious movement/thought, a shield from the enticement of risk.
A trench where soldiers get their limbs blown off.
A trench filled with your blood.
It's OK to lose a limb or two.
Only your head matters, and what's inside.
The knowledge locked therein.
The knowledge you spent years and hundreds of millions of dollars acquiring.
"THEY" are paying to suck it out of your skull and into the digital nether, where it can be transformed to valuable currency for the kings.
Knowing all this, firmly etched in your psyche, you wade through the blood filled trench.

"Training" (brainwashing) seemed like decades ago.
Had you aged.
Were you even alive.
You're burning in HELL.
The devil is fucking your ass in the morning and gutting you at night.

The blanket of extreme comfort has become another non-distinct fixture.
You pass it every day, and think "uh huh, there it is, whatever, FUCK."
It's a dreary reminder of why you wade through the blood.
Every. Monotonous. Day.

This is your routine:

You wake up.
You lay in bed staring at the ceiling.
You acknowledge the dread, the anxiety, the stomach pains, and the slight tension headache that will amass an army and beat your skull into submission later.
Maybe you do a workout, shoot some hoops, run, ride your bike, push-ups, squats.
Anything to escape the dread.
You stuff things into your mouth.

Evolution Can Suck It

Sustenance.
You shower, while trying to figure out what the day will bring.
Pain is a given, but what kind of pain.
You put on clothes to cover your shameful nakedness.
You check the clock.
You worry about arriving too early.
You worry about what kind of mood The Stress Monster will be in.
Fear wells inside of you at the thought, the unknown is torture.
The trick is to arrive either after or just as everyone else is, to avoid being the only target available.
The Stress Monster is almost always in a frantic bad mood.
But even the "good" moods are repulsive and highly toxic.
Either extreme is like nails being hammered through your balls by an incompetent carpenter, where he misses every few strikes and hits your ding dong.
9:45 am is the ideal arrival time.
It's not too early, not too late.
It's just fucking right.
You leave your house around 9:15 am.
It's a 15 to 20 minute drive.

You park your car.
You sit in your car and acknowledge the panic attack.
Some days you feel like you're about to die.
Others, not so much, you just hope to die.
You repeat to yourself, "why am I putting myself through this."
Extreme comfort follows as the reason, even though you're sick of it.
You walk in, slowly, keeping an eye out for someone you can team up with to take on The Stress Monster waiting to attack inside.
Usually there are no friendlies to be found.
You just hope someone's already inside taking the worst of the whipping.
The first one to arrive always gets the worst of it.
You scan your badge at the thing that prevents psychos from coming into the building and shooting everyone.
Enter your code for the door (1234).
You go through the security checkpoint.
Say "Hi" to the guard, who normally looks right through you, eyes trained on nothing in particular.
You walk through a big room filled with rows of tightly packed slaves wearing headset things tethered to telephones engaged in something called "technical support," aka "sales," aka "strong arming

morons to buy garbage," aka "a worse job than yours."
They're hawking the same garbage you're about to shovel from one pile to another, aka "the reason you're here."
You scan your badge again at another door.
The "technical support" slaves aren't allowed access to this part of the building.
Only the slaves with fancy, elaborate titles are allowed in here.
You walk through the door.
You look to the right, where your cube resides, rubbing its hands together diabolically in anticipation of your pain.
You glance at the blinds.
If they're open, he's there, pumping out wave after wave of stress.
If they're closed, there's a good chance he hasn't arrived...yet.
Every time you walk in and they're closed, it feels like God reaches down from Heaven, taps you on the shoulder with his enormous index finger, and says, "there ya go little buddy, I love you."
He raises his eyebrows and smiles while he says it, and then disappears back into the clouds.
The tension melts, you feel relaxed.
But those days are rare.

Most days he's there, pumping out powerful stress shock waves.
You listen and feel and cringe to the incessant clicking of keyboards.
Like chickens in coups pecking for grains sprinkled on plastic plates.
Sounds like razors across your balls, fingernails on a chalkboard, felt markers on cardboard.
The Stress Monster is the loudest, violently molesting the keys with his fat fingers, each stroke a defiant one, as if he's locked in a life or death duel with the computer.
He sighs just as violently.
Every few minutes, a panicked gasp for air followed by a tire being slashed.
The origin of the stress shock wave.
You put on your tattered armor and head towards your station.
Your cube is catty corner to his.
He can't see you coming, but his senses are so acute, he can feel when you're near.
He's always ready to pounce.
You try to sneak into your cube real quick to grab your water bottle, avoiding detection.
Most days you succeed.
Some days you fail.

Evolution Can Suck It

And on those failure days, you know you fucked up somehow.
Maybe you didn't answer a call from the server people in the middle of the night.
Maybe you did something that wasn't perfect, that wasn't done to his liking.
And during his obsessive compulsive ritual of checking up on you and everyone else EVERY SINGLE SECOND, he discovered your imperfection.
Or maybe he's just in an insanely jovial mood and wants to bludgeon your ears with enthusiastic talk about digital nonsense, technology minutiae, or how his Daddy (aka, "Napoleon," aka, "The Big Boss") was pleased in some way.
He lives to please his Daddy, often running into his office to tell him things like, "Daddy, look what I made the computer do," or, "Daddy, I'm a big boy, look at the poopy I made in my pants."
When Daddy is happy, he's happy.
When Daddy is pissy, he's even pissier.
And when he's pissy, he pisses on YOU and everyone else, his underlings, his servants, his infantry, his dogs to kick (slash) blame.
You grab your water bottle and pretend you don't hear or see him over in his little cube pounding away and sighing.

You head to the water fountain down the hall, passing by Daddy's office.
You peek in through your peripheral to see if he's there.
You pass other drones buzzing around, scurrying to keep up the illusion of biz-e-ness.
Hardly anyone acknowledges your existence.
They're too busy fighting the war.
The war you're about to have to get into the trenches and fight.
The war to turn a profit for the creator of this madness.
You squat down and fill your water bottle up.
You intentionally bought a big bottle, so it would take longer to fill up.
So that these little mini vacations might keep you from rolling grenades down the cubicle aisles.
As the water inches to the top, a recurring dream runs through your head.
The dream of one day quitting in dramatic fashion.
Like walking in with a wooden baseball bat and planting it between The Stress Monster's eyes.
Or being fired after spiral fracturing Daddy's arm because he tried to physically assault you for not being a perfect obedient flawless employee 24/7.
This fantasy comforts you in a way.

Evolution Can Suck It

It gives you the feeling of being in control, almost superior.
The adrenaline pumping through your veins may influence this feeling.
The high levels of stress an instinctual remnant from your days of fighting off wild beasts out to eat you.
These modern day wild beasts, whose names appear in boxes above yours, are out to kill you.
Their indifference to your well being is infuriating.
Violent imagery is your only comfort.
Water bottle full, you casually stroll back to the trench.
Along the way, you mentally prepare as best you can for the day's assault.
Which enemy will be most ferocious today.
You sit down, sigh, and stare at the gray cube wall.
"Hello <censored>."
This is your routine.

2.

You roll your chair into the meeting, aka "beat down," position.
The three other team members roll their chairs into position.
You hold your full water bottle on your knee.

You'll most likely finish it before this daily meeting, aka "daily beat down," is complete.
It's your shield, a thing to do to dissipate nervous energy.
The same nervous energy that induced the panic attack earlier in your car.
It's the anticipation of the nervous energy possibly suffocating you at this moment that causes the panic.
A vicious feedback loop.
You take a couple sips of water.

The Stress Monster launches in to Red about some boring thing he's supposed to be making progress on.
Red is your buddy.
You've been drunk with Red.
You've been to professional sports games with Red.
You've watched Red ingest mood altering substances.
You're friends, in an odd sort of way.
Deeper than just work mates, but no deeper than getting drunk buddies.

Red replies, saying something negative, like, "I can't do that thing you want me to do because A) I don't give a shit, B) you could hire a chicken to do

it, and C) FUCK YOU DO IT YOURSELF ASSHOLE."
The Stress Monster says, in a single panicked breathed, something like, "you need to have that done by the end of the day so Daddy and Lisp Boy won't get mad at me and spank me and send me to my room without desert."
He takes a big gulp of air immediately after the word "desert."

Lisp Boy is Daddy's boss.
You've talked to him maybe once.
More like, you passed him in the hall and said "hi" to him and he looked at you like you had a purple horn growing out of your face.
You sat down at a table with him and the other boss people during your first week and ate food together, so you think it appropriate to acknowledge his existence whenever you see him.
He doesn't feel the same towards you, probably because he's a FUCK HOLE.

The Stress Monster expels the smoking round he just fired at Red and chambers another.
Your heart races, anticipating he'll aim at you next.
"Uhhhhhhhhhhh," he stammers while searching for his next victim.

"THAD," he screams.
Everyone jumps a little.
The Stress Monster asks something like, "what's the status of that stupid thing you're supposed to be working on."

Thad is the really smart guy, with a non-repulsive personality (a rare combination).
He's a content little drone, highly risk averse, at home being subservient.
You are work mates, but really nothing more.
You've had beers with Thad and bitched about being workers in the same shitty situation.
You figure he's pretty much a shut in when he's not chained to the computer, but likable enough as someone you have to work next to every day.
At the very least, you have little desire to split his head open with an ax.

Thad responds to The Stress Monster with words like "generated," and "weird," and "differential," and "routines," and other big ones strung together in a way only a robot could produce.
His ability to make you feel supremely stupid through language is erotic.
Your eyes glaze over while Thad and The Stress Monster interact in an excited exchange.

Evolution Can Suck It

They're like digital soul mates, humanoid brothers in arms, sequential serial numbers.
Sometimes you imagine them in the bathroom's handicap stall beating off (synchronously) to pictures of solid state hard drives and Fibonacci sequences.
Which is weird, because they don't get along very well.
Thad has confided in you that he doesn't like the Stress Monster too much, and that he'd much rather have Daddy as his master instead.
You tend to agree with him.

You realize it's about your turn to face the firing squad.
The Stress Monster expels the round fired at Thad and chambers another.
He looks at you, sighs, and says, without taking a new breath, something like, "how's the fix for the stupid thing to upgrade the other boring thing coming along."
He inhales violently after the word "along."

You feel the bullet enter your chest.
It burns, and your heart panics, pumping red hot lava through your veins.
Your head tightens, your hands and feet tingle.

You feel like you're glowing hot, your ears the tips of lit matches.
Perspiration flows in an attempt to maintain normal temperature.
You open your mouth, stalling to find the proper response, "uhhhhhhhhhh."
You say some words you think make sense, but you can't be sure.
Your mouth's a slave to the lizard controlling your brain.
You take a deep breath, remind yourself that none of this matters.
A few more sips, water is half gone.

"Ok, I needed you to finish that yesterday. Why isn't it done."
His tone is authoritative, enraging.
"BECAUSE I FUCKING HATE THIS FUCKING JOB AND YOUR FUCKING COCK SUCKING FAT FUCK FACE," you think but don't say.
You want to pick up your chair and ram it into his bloated head.
You want to bury a hunting knife in his sternum.
You want to tape his hands and feet together and pour boiling oil down his throat until he bursts into flames from the inside out.

Evolution Can Suck It

Your heart is racing in preparation for the fight.
Conflict is a daily occurrence, yet you haven't adapted.
You stare back into his blank gaze, burning a hole through his fat head with your fury.
He breaks the silence, saying something about fearing his Daddy, implying that it will be your fault if Daddy gets mad at him.

You decide not talking is a good strategy.
You've tried the explaining reality to him strategy on several occasions, and the result is always the same.
There's never a good excuse for your failure to maintain perfection.
He doesn't understand the limitations of the human body and mind.
He can't be reasoned, bargained, or negotiated with.
He isn't looking for resolution anyway.
He's looking to light a fire under your ass, because he fears the wrath of Daddy.
He's trying to force his irrational urgency on to you, so he can deflect Daddy's wrath into your lap.

You continue staring into his blank face.
You could fry an egg on his forehead.

He looks disheveled, frustrated, frazzled, and stressed out.
It's his normal appearance.
"You need to get it out today."
"Ok, whatever," you say.
He takes a rushed deep breath and sighs in disgust, signaling he's not finished berating.
"I mean Daddy has been asking about it and I have to give him a status update before noon today and he's not going to be happy if it's not done," he sucks another breath like he just surfaced from the ocean after almost drowning.
"Ok, I can't create time, or magically stop it somehow," you say, knowing your defiance will further anger him.
Red snickers.

The Stress Monster's face flushes with blood.
You can literally see the aneurism forming.
He has no good response for you, so he surrenders with a threat, "OK, well I'm going to tell Daddy it's not finished."
"Great," you say.

He thinks you fear the wrath of Daddy.
You do.
Slightly.

Evolution Can Suck It

But your hope for being forcefully liberated from this pathetic existence outweighs any fear.

Your body slumps.
A small victory for your pride, a crushing defeat for your sanity.
You roll your chair back in to the slave position, affix the shackles, pick up your weapon, and begin the battle.

YOU GET IN TROUBLE BECAUSE OF A GUY NAMED "TED"

1.

You've never met the guy you call "Ted."
But he calls you on occasion.
Usually in the middle of the night.
Usually to report bad news, something that's gone wrong with the computers you're slave to.
That's his duty, his assigned function in life, his only reason to continue breathing.
God's beautiful creation.

His name isn't really "Ted."
The woman who pushed him out named him something else, something you can't remember and don't care to.
But he sounds like a "Ted," and does things like a "Ted" would do them, and you imagine him looking like a "Ted" might look.

"Ted," the ordinary worker man.
The guy who wakes you up in the middle of the night to talk about computer problems.

He thumbs the edge of the table he sits at, smoothing out an imaginary imperfection, waiting anxiously for the computers to go wrong.
There are others in the room with him.
They have names like "Bob," and "Dan," and "Tony."
They take turns letting words slide out of their mouths and run down their chins.
There's a stagnant pool of words on the floor, waiting to be consumed and formed into new words.
This is their version of conversation.
Drooling words on the floor.
This is one of the things they do to pass the time between stuff going wrong.

"Ted" has his right hand on a mouse tethered to a computer.
Thus, tethering "Ted" to the computer, leaving no question who is in control.
(Hint: The machines are.)
He pushes his index finger down and the mouse emits a [click] sound.

Evolution Can Suck It

The computer illuminates a different sequence of lights.
"Ted's" eyes dart around the new stimulus.
The grey matter contained in his head churns through routine, systematically, robotically processing the fresh information.

He's slouched down in a plush, leather-like chair; his head snuggled into the pillowy top.
Aside from the movement of his eyes and his right index finger, he's motionless, catatonic.
Consciousness isn't necessary.
He does as the machines tell him to do.
Machine says, "everything is OK, 'Ted,' do nothing."
"Ted" does nothing.
Machine says, "something is wrong, 'Ted,' do this thing."
"Ted" does whatever thing it tells him to do, without question.

Another [click].
Uh, oh.
The machine tells him to dial the number that belongs to you.

FONZI BROWNWOOD

2.

Your phone rings.
You know who it is without looking.
Fucking "Ted."
"FUCK THAT GUY," you say in your head.
You debate letting it ring.
But you know The Stress Monster's retribution is more repulsive than his daily mania.

He's what they call the "secondary."
This is the person who is the fall back to the "primary" (you).
The "secondary" gets called if the "primary" doesn't answer.
He's always your "secondary."
Because one weekend when you were "primary," you ignored "Ted's" attempts to reach you, punting responsibility to whoever was your "secondary" at the time.
The Stress Monster expressed his anger at your indifference by sending you nasty threats via every form of digital communication that exists on planet Earth.
All weekend long, like clockwork, he'd send you things like, "why aren't you answering," and "I'm

Evolution Can Suck It

very disappointed in your behavior," and "this is unacceptable," and "I'm telling my Daddy."
He's always keeping a watchful eye for anything that might upset Daddy.
His life revolves around pleasing Daddy.
And you ignoring your responsibilities upset his need for making sure Daddy doesn't punish him.
"Fuck him," you said to yourself, as you sat in a comfortable chair in front of electronic distraction and watched his angry threats pass through your skull.
So now, as punishment, he's always your "secondary."

You decide to answer.
"Hmm...huh...uhhh...what, yeah," you say.
It's 2:15 am.
"Ted" says, "hi, this is *<who gives a fuck, some disposable human>*. Hey, this machine is telling me something is wrong with it."
"Huh, what the fuck that does mean."
"Umm, this thing isn't working right. That's what it says."
The words just slide right out of his mouth.
He sounds like a fat eighth grader drooling in front of a TV eating a bucket of ice cream and watching cartoons.

You know "Ted" isn't capable of conscious thought.
You know he can't solve any problems on his own.
You know that he expects you to get up and make an effort to fix what's broken.
Instead of doing that, you say, "I don't know. I can't do anything. Call the Stress Monster," then hang up.

2 minutes pass.

You realize what you've done.
The words "FUCK" and "ME" blink in red lights inside your eye lids.
It's 2:20 am.

You were supposed to get up out of your comfortable bed and pretend to give a shit.
You were supposed to deeply care about serving the machines.
You were supposed to respond like a good soldier.
A soldier ready to sacrifice his life.
Your life.
The only life you have.
Take the fucking shrapnel, the bullets, the knife, the anger, aggression, and stress.
For the glory of the company.

Evolution Can Suck It

You're disposable.
You're sacrificial.
You're obedient.
"How high would you like me to jump, massa' sir."
But you hung up.
You deflected the problem, yet again.
You did so unconsciously.
Who's fucking conscious at 2:15 am.
Vampires, drug dealers, and prostitutes.

You can't sleep now.
The ceiling drips horrific scenarios into your mind.
The anticipation for what awaits you in the morning is agonizing.
The devil smiles and prepares the burning pitchfork for your morning impaling.
"FUCK" and "ME."

3.

The Stress Monster lectures you on the pain he suffered through last night because you told "Ted" to fuck off.
He uses words like, "responsibility," and "dedication," and "principles," and "work ethic."
Words that bounce off you and fall flat to the ground.

FONZI BROWNWOOD

You hang your head in defeat as his panicked words penetrate your psyche, lighting up all the systems in your body that produce deadly toxins.
Doesn't he realize you're already dead.
You're floating into Heaven and he's trying to grab you by the ankles to slow your ascent.

Every day is similar to this one.
You're not always the target of his fury, but even the splash damage of someone else being whipped is enough to cause searing pain.
And even though you are not responsible for the machine's temperament, you are an accomplice.
You're expected to catch every little nuance.
Every possible scenario.
Every tiny little thing that could go wrong.

In some third world country, there's a man riding a goat home from a shitty job.
He's beaten down, after having worked 15 hours answering phones and dealing with over privileged, whiny, spoiled first world people.
Because of your imperfect existence as a human, he was unable, at 2:15 am your time, to buy a stupid thing from the company that's enslaved you.

Evolution Can Suck It

A thing that might (most likely won't) improve his life by a sliver.
At least for the moment, he would've had some escape, some sense of accomplishment.

You fucked that experience up for him.
You failed HIM.
You failed EARTH, all of HUMANITY.
It's highly likely, using the ferocity of The Stress Monster's verbal beating as a barometer, that society has been ruined because of this failure.
Because of YOUR FAILURE.
Wars are about to break out.
The ground is going to open up and let the demons from Hell loose.
The Apocalypse is upon us all.
All because a machine wasn't operating perfectly for half a millisecond.

The man in the third world country, who will now have to slaughter his only beloved goat to survive, hit the unhappy machine at just the right time.
At 2:15 am.
Which triggered "Ted" to push the button labeled "End Existence on Earth."

You take a deep breathe and say nothing.

You raise your eyes to The Stress Monster's, only to be greeted with that familiar emotionless gaze. That 1,000 yard stare.
He's breathing like he just finished a 15 round prize fight to the death.
An image of you plunging a sword into his abdomen flashes through your mind.

You break the staring contest, get up out of your chair, and go for a walk outside.

YOU BECOME PART OF THE SPECTACLE

1.

A drone with a stupid mouth tells you it's probably going to be cold.
So you buy a cashmere sweater.
It was on sale at some cut rate clothes store.
You got cashmere because the drone with the stupid fucking mouth also said to dress nice.
And because cashmere makes you feel (superficially) like royalty.
Two birds with one stone.
Fancy and functional.
You take a moment to admire your brilliant mind.

Actually, the drone with the fucking stupid mouth used the words "dress appropriately."
It made it a point to emphasize those two words to you.

Otherwise, you might dress in your usual homeless style: ripped shorts, flip flops, and some kind of ill fitting t-shirt with "ironic" or "funny" graphics on it.
Where "you might" = "you most definitely with 100% certainty would."

They couldn't have that.
An uncaring, drunk, social retard running around dressed like Fred the homeless hobo.
The more elite humans attending the party would be appalled.
They can't be seen next to a vagabond.
They need to look good in case they're photographed, and that photograph somehow makes it into some well read publication that no one with half a brain gives a fuck about.
It would ruin their image if they were seen fraternizing with "commoners."
So you decide to conform and "dress appropriately."
Mostly, because the drone with the fucking stupid mouth threatened you.
It said something like, "the meat heads hired to protect the image of the people who give a shit won't let you in if you don't 'dress appropriately.'"

Evolution Can Suck It

You were given two tickets, even though you're going by yourself.
You don't have a date.
You NEVER have a date.
One of your friend's friends once dubbed you "solo vino."
That's Spanish, or Italian, or something that means "always alone."
You figure women are so repulsed by you that your odds of securing a date in the future seem slim.
But you got an extra ticket because there are two free drink things attached to it.
So now you have 4 free drinks.
You feel empowered somehow, like you beat The System.
You showed them.
It's like you're stealing from the God's of imbibing, who charge a premium for such a privilege (as to become imbibed).
You plan on paying that premium tonight.
And you're sticking it to The System by having two extra free drinks.

2.

You arrive via cab.
You pay the man who drove it an exorbitant fee.

The expense of this party is vast.
You've already paid a hefty sum of your own blood for the right to be in attendance.
Your labor, transformed into this, the corporate spectacle of the year.
A spectacle you're about to be a part of.

You're on the inside thrusting your groin area at the crowds gathered outside looking on in envy.
"Ohhh, wooooooow, look at that," they'll think in amazement.
"I want to be inside there, gyrating my baby maker and rubbing elbows with fringe celebrities."
You stare at them like a beaten down, hung over coal miner.
You know the toll they would have to pay to be in your shoes.
A bucket of blood, some drips of tears and sweat, and a dash of dignity.
Blend well, pour into the machine, and 365 days later, out comes this "incredible" spectacle.
An occasion rivaled by no other in the era of corporate dominance.
A "perk" of the job.
A distraction device.
"Fill 'em with booze and shitty entertainment, and toss money into the air. Watch 'em grabbin' for it,

and fallin' all over each other in greedy denial, and I'll become the richest human alive," you imagine the purveyor of this spectacle (Ego) thinking to himself as he emerges from a fake smoke and generic laser light show.

He's on an elevated stage, about 10 feet in the air, above the drooling masses.
The masses he's leveraging to be in such a position, lording superficially above them.
10 feet being some kind of golden ratio.
Not too high to be pretentious, but high enough to produce the illusion of possessing exponentially more significance than the "commoners" on regular ground, who are oblivious.
They worship him as God, like slaves grateful for a day free of beatings.
He is their master, the reason they are here, on the inside, thrusting their groin area at everyone envious of their privilege.

You're standing in line, waiting to cash in one of your free drink tickets, soaking it all in.
"Wow, he's sooo cool," you overhear someone saying to a person standing next to them.
"Ha ha, Ego always has to make an entrance," someone else says.

You're not impressed.
You're jealous.
Jealous of Ego's success.
Jealous of his wannabe rock star attitude, his "I'll do whatever the fuck I want" swagger.
You want to be like him.
You want to be in his position, elevated above the drooling masses and parading around with hot girls on YOUR arm, pretending to be a big deal.
But you're standing in line with the other sweat hogs, anonymously, waiting to indulge in the distraction.
Your consumer instincts are strong.
You possess the great ability to be easy prey.
You lack the qualities necessary to strut among the manufactured clouds of smoke.

"I'll have a dirty water," you tell the bartender.
"What's that," she asks.
"Do you have Hennessey."
"No. We have whiskey, vodka, and gin."

You contemplate for a moment, knowing damn well she wouldn't know what a "dirty water" is. There are only 3 people on the planet that know what it is, and one of them is you.

Evolution Can Suck It

This super secret insider knowledge makes you feel cool, important somehow, like you're an exclusive member of some underground club that turns its nose up to mainstream stuff.
But you're no good at keeping secrets.
You're destroying the club by giving away all its secrets.

"Give me a whiskey and 7," you tell the bartender, pretending to be perturbed by her ignorance of "dirty water."
As she's pouring your drink, she asks, "what's a 'dirty water?'"
"Well, the technical term is Hennessey separated. It's Hennessey, milk, and Kahlua, and when poured right, they all separate in the glass," you respond.
The irony is so thick.
You feel yourself drifting into territory you despise.
You feel aloof, like you were setting her up for that question before you even opened your mouth.
You knew she would ask.
You were hoping she would ask, so you could educate her.
So you could spill some more of the super secret club's secrets.
These are the same qualities you despise in others.

And here you are, wallowing in the same filthy behavior, relishing the power.
You take your drink.

3.

You're in a building that hosts a professional sports team.
It has one of those retractable roofs.
It's closed.
And it's fucking hot.
You're wearing slacks, a long sleeve dress shirt, a tie (noose) and your newly acquired cashmere sweater.
And you're balls and armpits are leaking fluid like a fat guy eating a bucket of flaming hot chicken wings.
The stupid fucking drone with the mouth lied to you.
You feel deceived, but you're so accustomed to it, you barely register a head shake.

The theme of the spectacle is something like, "circus night," or "carnival days," or "redneck fun times."
Whatever.
There is a big Ferris wheel as the center piece.

Evolution Can Suck It

A working Ferris wheel, filled with people riding in vertical circles.
Up.
Down.
Round and round.
<insert some clever metaphor about life here>

The line to ride it is ridiculously long.
People seem eager to flow in circles, going nowhere.
Digging the rut a little deeper with each revolution.
The metaphor so apparent it's laughing at everyone in plain view.

There are also bumper cars, and other carnival style games.
Like ring toss, where, at a real carnival, the rings are impossibly small.
But here, they are big enough so everyone wins.

There's also a game where you shoot water into a clown's mouth and it makes a horse thing slide up.
Clowns + horses seems like a reasonable combination.
Whatever.
It's a race to the top against the other players.
You pick up the water gun.

A buzzer sounds.
You shoot the water directly into the clown's mouth.
It's easy, and you win.

Your prize is a stuffed animal.
For one second in your life, in this life, in this miserable existence you've entombed yourself in, you feel exonerated.
You feel like an accomplished person, a winner.
And you debate whether or not this is all by design.
Just another element in the distraction.
Make everyone feel like a winner, even if it's fixed, and they'll give another year of their life shoveling gold into Ego's bloated head.
Winning makes everything feel better.
It makes pain easier to tolerate.
It makes everything taste better, look better, sound better.
And being drunk helps also.
It's hard to say "NO" to someone who empowers you to be a winner AND feeds you alcohol mixed with a good time.

You take your prize, a medium sized, generic looking stuffed animal.

Evolution Can Suck It

You get back in line for another go.

Four victories and an armful of stuffed animals later, the operators ask you to not play any more.
At a job, dominating the competition is frowned upon.
It breeds resentment.
The dominated will band together and drag the dominator down to their level.
Or, they just beat him to death, starting at the genitals, and then eat his face off while he's still conscious.
You can sense the armies amassing against you.
Time for another free drink.

4.

A generic sounding cover band is playing an obnoxious song that claims they "don't need nuthin' but a good time."
They keep singing those words over and over.
They're on the elevated stage, dancing and jumping around, feigning enthusiasm, pretending to be the once successful band they're imitating.

The scene reminds you of the small lounges scattered around the big casinos in the city of sin.

You used to walk by them while searching for..."a good time."
That city has a reputation of consuming identities, individuality, and any sense of purpose.
This spectacle you're buried in has that same feel to it.
Like you're a drifter, meandering through the night, aimless, only there because it's there.
This is what it's like BEING the spectacle, instead of merely witnessing it.
It's like being an actor in a clever commercial.
To the audience, it's funny and cool and appealing.
To the actor, she sees all the levers, and wires, and smoke and mirrors, and all the little pieces of film cut from the final version piled on the floor.
Then she realizes her whole existence is captured on the rejected film.
The commercial, to her, becomes an abomination.

The bartender tilts his head back and raises his eyebrows, the universal signal for "what'll you have."
"Whiskey and coke, please," you say.
You break off another glossy, colorful drink ticket and hand it to the bartender.
So much care and artistic talent wasted creating these gorgeous tickets.

Evolution Can Suck It

Your appreciation of its beauty lasts as long as the time it takes to lift your fingers from its surface. Disposable art.

You have two stuffed animals tucked under each arm.
You notice other people carrying similar amounts of stuffed animals.
You thought your victories were special.
You make your way through the crowd, again, meandering aimlessly.
No one looks familiar, and even the ones that do refuse to acknowledge you.
You lift your eyebrows and tilt your head back to them, the universal sign for, "what's up."
They divert their eyes down and away, the universal sign for, "FUCK, I hope that person who I totally know didn't see me. I don't want to talk to him."
Whatever.

You discover a roped off area.
Not roped off by that cheap looking nylon security gate stuff you find at the airport.
This is the good stuff.
If it had been invented in the time when kings ruled the land, they would've used it in their castles.

It's plush, red velvet style, connected together with gold coated poles.
Probably not real gold, just gold color.
Another fucking illusion.

Inside the red velvet ropes, there's chefs wearing paper top hats and carving some kind of meat for the honored guests.
Some of the honored guests you recognize.
You see <censored>, whose face you decorated during "training" (brainwashing).
She's wearing a white evening dress.
Looks like she might also be a bonafide midget.

You're hungry, and all the other spots to eat looked like garbage.
But this looks luxurious.
So you make your way around, following the velvet rope like a wolf tracking a bleeding...whatever the fuck they eat.

At the entrance, you find two very large men dressed in black tuxedos.
They're wearing little things in their right ears, connected to a curly cord that disappears into their jackets.

They look intimidating, and they're staring off, above the crowd, trying not to make eye contact with anyone.
They're like two terminators waiting, hoping for someone to cause them trouble so they can exercise their might.

You approach as if you belong.
Like a steel door slamming shut, the two ear thing wearing slabs of meat come together to block your path.
One of them holds out his hand to stop you from entering.
Neither says a word.
They don't have to.
You know what's up.
This area is reserved for the special super elite, the important people who grace the elevated stage.
This is their holding pen, where they're lavished with fine food, expensive wine, and engaging conversation.
They use words like, "me too," and "oh, yeah," and "hmmm, that's interesting."

You see Daddy walking around inside.
He's walking towards you, seemingly making eye contact.

Seemingly going to part the large men like butt cheeks and allow you entrance.
But at the last minute he stops, turns to his right, and begins talking with someone.
Not even a "hi," or "hey," or "fuck you fuck face, fuck off."
The big shit dick shoved right in your face.

You get the hint, standing in knowing confusion, staring in disbelief at one of the large men, four stuffed animals and a whiskey and coke monopolizing the free use of your arms.
You think briefly about just barging in.
No way you get past these two meat curtains.
And even if you do, you're fucked.
Terminators NEVER quit, they NEVER stop, and they're ALWAYS looking to kill.
You don't have that kind of stamina.

You stagger off in disgust, going over scenario after scenario where you come out a victor.
Where you overtake the velvet rope area single handedly, kill everyone inside with your bare hands, take the stage and declare victory over tyranny.
Everyone rejoices and praises you as their savior.
Thank you, Jesus.

Evolution Can Suck It

But in real life, you slink into the abyss, blending back in with the commoners.
Commoners who live by the equation: do nothing + say nothing = be nothing.
It's too fucking easy to be nothing.
This is where you belong.

5.

You crack off the last glossy drink ticket and prepare it for the bartender.
It has a black background, with colorful fireworks, an artistic rendition of a Ferris wheel, and it's emblazoned with the corporate symbol.
"This is my oppression," you think as you stare at the ticket, "the device of my enslavement, the comfort of intoxication."
And intoxication has arrived, after three stout drinks.
The peak has been climbed, the flag of conquest planted.
But you want to go higher.
So in addition to the free drink, you order a second.

Your corporate master, the creator of your prison, is on stage reading names.

Your drinks arrive.
"$7," the bartender says.
You pull out a $20 bill and give it to her.
She makes change and you drop $2 into the tip jar.
Now, you're paying the company to work for them.
You're giving them their money back, with interest.
They contend that they can only "legally" give you two free drinks.
But you believe that's just a ploy, like a drug dealer offering free drugs with the realistic hope that you'll become a regular paying customer.
You're just the type of person to become a regular paying customer.

"Fred Tamarillo," Ego reads into the microphone.
Fred just won $500, for no other reason than existing on Earth, breathing air, and being named Fred Tamarillo, worker drone at company X.
Not for being a superior worker man.
Not for saving the Earth from Genghis Khan or Godzilla.
Nope.
He won because his name was printed on a piece of paper, thrown into a hopper, and selected by one of the hot girl props on stage.
"Susan meela, milla, milla, knock, a, son."
He says it like he has a mouthful of dicks.

Evolution Can Suck It

You deposited your stuffed animals at a table occupied by some of the people who you have to interact with sometimes during working hours.
They didn't invite you to join them.
You forced your way into their social stagnation.
The significance of your victories shooting water into a clown's mouth was reduced to rubble when you saw a pile of stuffed animals already on the center of the table.
In the corporate world, there is no path that leads to significance.
A worker's victories must be averaged into every other worker's victories.
And that average has to come close to the victories contained in the computation of that average.
There is no bell curve.
There is simply a straight line, with slight (microscopic) deviations.
"Remarkable" is measured in millimeters instead of miles.
Striving for "remarkable" is discouraged.
The stuffed animals already residing on the center of the table a sweet analogy to this law of average.

You make your way back to the table you're unwelcome at.

"Gavin Escolander."
Each name read a reminder that hard work is moot. You already lost when you signed up to be one of Ego's pawns.

You sit down.
"Fuckin' read my name you asshole," you yell at the stage.
You're a drunken mess.
"Fuckin' read it, bitch."
People turn around and look at you.
You leer back at them, daring them to confront you.
You feel brave in this environment, amongst the minions of order takers, the cube dwellers, the confrontational averse.
THE FUCKING SLAVES.
The very people you've come to hate.
The people you wish to escape.
The person you are.
The person you hate.
The person you're trying in vain to kill with free drinks.
You're willing to sacrifice your money at the same alter you collected it from, to murder the slave inside of you.
You're antagonizing strangers to beat it out of you.

Evolution Can Suck It

"So, having fun," Employee #9 (whatever his fucking name is) asks you with a smirk on his stupid face.
His name's been read 3 times already.
God loves him more than you.
3 times more.
He's the antithesis to The Stress Monster, who's sitting across the table next to a lady you assume he has shoved his penis in a time or two.

You'd rather have Employee #9 as the person who is your daily dictator.
He's the lesser of multiple evils, you suppose.
Until this moment, neither he nor The Stress Monster has uttered a single word to you.
Other than a head nod when you dropped off your stuffed animals, they've given you no proof you're even here right now.

Employee #9 came on an airplane from some other place.
The company flew him in, along with everyone else who lives in a different part of the world.
Just so you could all pretend to be one big happy family.
For one night.

Where "happy family" = "group of people with fake smiles, occupying the same location, facing the same direction, doing the same things."

You're sitting next to a girl who has been claimed by someone else.
Information you will come to learn in a few minutes.
But at the moment, she's a cute girl sitting next to you aching to have you bless her with flirty conversation.
That's what the alcohol is telling you.
Intoxication has a way of coloring reality in your favor.
From your perspective, everyone is aching for your attention.
And who are you to deprive them of such joy.

"Half these girls are hired," you say to her.
She looks at you confused, and nods, and says, "Ooooooh, K."
"They're hookers," you clarify.
"Yeah, maybe."
"Like this one," you point at a cute little girl in a silver, very short skirt, just long enough to cover her butt cheeks.
"I bet he paid at least $300 for that."

Evolution Can Suck It

She nods in agreement and fakes a smile.

In your state, you're killing it.
She's in to you.
She's totally immersed in this deep conversational bludgeoning about hookers.
Briefly, you imagine taking her home and fucking her like the rock star you are.
Pulling her hair, slapping her ass.
And she loves it, of course.
"What do you think," you finally ask for her opinion.
"I don't know, I guess."
Insightful.

She turns and looks at the stage, pretending to enjoy the has-been blues band that hasn't tasted relevancy in a long, long time.
"These guys suck," you say.
She ignores you.
"You wanna go ride the Ferris wheel with me," you ask.
"Uhh, she's claimed, buddy," some guy sitting next to her interrupts your attempts at drunken romance.
A guy you totally didn't realize was there.
Intoxication also creates tunnel vision.

In your memories, all you see is her face, surrounded by blurry images.
Then his face, leaning over her to say the thing he said, protecting his territory.

You focus back on her and raise your eyebrows, indicating the question still stands.
"Soooooooo, is that a no."

6.

"Let's go to a strip club," some random guy in the line you're standing in to go home says.
You can barely focus, the alcohol corrupting your ability to be normal.
The washed up blues band is still pumping out songs from the days when a handful of people cared they existed.
All their songs sound exactly alike.
You can't tell where one ends and another begins.
You can hear the sound waves echoing off the buildings where you're standing.

"Ok, were we goin'," you ask, wobbling and hiccuping.
The guy looks at you like you just landed on Earth.
His glassy eyes staring right through you.

Evolution Can Suck It

He turns to the people he's standing with and says, "let's go to Bung Holes."
You agree, inviting yourself to be a part of their gang.

This is typical drunk behavior for you.
You're like an invasive social leech, glomming on to whatever group is near you.
Except this group is about to crush your hopes of having a meaningful, debaucherous afterhours escapade.

Their cab arrives.
You nonchalantly follow them and attempt to get in.
They completely ignore you.
Just as you're about to crawl in, they close the door and drive off.
"What the fuck assholes," you scream at the cab driving off.

You've become that one drunken guy.
The guy that crashes the party, says some things no one likes, pisses in the fish bowl, breaks a few windows, mugs down with someone's wife, takes a shit on the bed, then vomits into the toilet with the lid down and passes out in it.

All the people you work adjacent to are staring at you.

From their perspective, you're an asshole.
You're the guy they can shake their head at and say, "at least I'm not THAT drunk."
Because being less of a bad thing is a good thing.

From your perspective, they're all assholes conspiring to kill you.

You direct a threatening "whad'r you lookin' at," at your audience.
You turn away and mumble "faggots" under your breathe.
Your cab pulls up.
You get in and the driver turns around and looks at you, waiting for direction.
The words "Bung" and "Holes" slide out of your mouth.

7.

You wake up the next morning on the cold tile floor of your condo, using your cashmere sweater as a pillow.

Evolution Can Suck It

You're fully clothed, trying to remember how the fuck you got here.
You're trying to piece together what happened between the cab ride to "Bung Holes" and right now.
Your head is pounding.
Your mind is racing.
All the possibilities, the consequences, the possibility of shame and humiliation.
SHIT, Monday morning is a few hours away.

You scrape yourself off the floor.
The ritual seems all too familiar.

YOU LIBERATE YOURSELF

1.

Quitting a shitty job is like crawling out of your own grave.
It's like drowning yourself and having your best friend resuscitate you.
It's like taking a long, hot shower after being raped at knife point.

You fantasized about leaving and never coming back.
You imagined the pleasure of ignoring the frantic calls from The Stress Monster.
You fantasized about responding to his angry sounding texts of "where r u" with something like, "beating my wet dick on a frozen pole in Antarctica to see if it will stick."
Or, "seeing how many golf balls I can stuff in my mouth."
Or, "thinking about you, and wondering where it all went wrong...I <3 U."

FONZI BROWNWOOD

The law of obedience says two weeks notice is the
proper thing to give when quitting a job.
It keeps your record "clean."
It's the professional thing to do.
It's what normal, average, everyday, ordinary employees do.
But you're not any of those things.
You're a rebel, remember.

You get out of your car and walk towards the door.
The fear tries to hold you back.
You feel like you're walking in mud.
But you keep putting one foot in front of the other.
Forward.

You get to the front door, take a deep breath.
Your body is screaming to reconsider your plan.
You walk past the disinterested security guard, who
looks at you out of routine then immediately returns to mindless digital occupation.

You walk through the call center.
All these souls, trapped in mediocrity, spinning
their wheels, following the rut.
All of the sudden you feel sanctimonious.

Evolution Can Suck It

You want to erect a makeshift pulpit and preach
the virtue of the action you're about to take.
If only the panic would subside long enough to
string together coherent thought.
If only these impossibly ignorant drones were open
to your message.

You step through the next security door.
The blast of stress thumps your chest.
Your body tenses.
Your mind races.
You debate for a fraction of a second turning
around and running away.
It's your normal response to danger.
RUN AWAY YOU FUCKING IDIOT.
But you march forward.

The blinds are open.
The Stress Monster's keyboard is smoking, the
gears of progress grinding along.
You can hear him huffing and puffing.
You feel your heart beating against your sternum.

You cross the threshold of his awareness.
He spins around in his chair and says, "Hey. How
was your trip."

As the word "trip" slips past his lips, you press the barrel of your imaginary shotgun against his head. You squeeze the trigger.

In a blink, all your anxiety and fear and stress and frustrations and anger explode through his fat head.
You watch in slow motion the fragments of his skull and brains paint the cubicle walls.
The force of the blast satisfies every particle of your body.
Immediately, you feel at peace, like you've been born again.

You stand there for a second or two.
The barrel of your imaginary shotgun smokes.
You take a deep breath, inhaling the aroma of vindication, freedom.
You kneel down beside him and whisper, "I quit."

It was too easy, boring even.
You take off your slave badge and rest it on his motionless chest.
You say, "goodbye."

You walk outside and breathe.
The air tastes cleaner.

Evolution Can Suck It

The sun feels warmer, friendlier.
Your body relaxes, relieved and thankful to still be alive.

ACT THREE

THINGS THAT HAPPEN WHEN EVOLUTION PUTS YOU INSIDE JOSEPH SMITH'S BUTT HOLE

YOU GET THROWN INTO A CAGE

1.

You're sent to a place to work in a trailer parked in a dark garage.
A dark garage that feels like someone (probably multiple someones) might have been murdered in.

The trailer that sits in this dark garage has a thousand locks, a security camera, and an eerie presence.
It has no air conditioning.
You don't even have access to the trailer because you don't have the right credentials.
Credentials that some guy wearing a badge and a gun and maybe a fake mustache must "bless" you with.

You sit in the visitor cube.

Because you don't have access to the trailer where you need to work.
Because the guy with the badge hasn't made the determination if you're worthy or not of the proper credentials to have access.
Because you're a flawed fucking human.
And only un-flawed fucking humans get access.
"I'm fucked," you think.

The small cubicle you're sitting in allows you to see everyone else sitting in identical cubicles.
They're all doing the exact same thing: sitting down facing a computer monitor.
The exact same thing you're doing.

You see a lady sitting directly across from you.
She's old, staring like a zombie into her monitor.
You imagine her when she was young, and how many dicks she sucked.
You're doing all this because you have nothing to really do.
The instructions, "look busy, make it seem like you care, play the part," circulate through your head.
But all you can think about are all those dicks, all stuffed into her mouth at once, all coming at the same time.

Evolution Can Suck It

You return your eyes to stare at your computer monitor.
If a photographer were to come in and take a snapshot of the entire office, everyone would look exactly the same.
You'd all have the exact same face, facing into your monitors.
Working.
"This ain't fucking work," you think.
"This is slavery. I'm a SLAVE. WHY THE FUCK AM I HERE."
You scream at yourself in your head.

You look over your shoulder at one of your bosses sitting in the corner.
He's sitting there, motionless, slumped in his chair, wearing a bright green shirt.
His eyes are pointed at his computer monitor, like everyone else.
Like you should be doing, because they pay you to sit here slumped in this cushy office chair and stare at the computer monitor, and type on the keyboard occasionally.
But you don't have a reason to.
Because the guy wearing a badge, who is responsible for giving out the thing that gives you access to the eerie trailer, hasn't done yours yet.

And the lady that is supposed to know this stuff knows it, but at the same time doesn't.
And the guy, who is your boss also, but in a different office at this moment, doesn't know it either.
Because the lady that's supposed to know it hasn't told him, because she doesn't really know it either.
But she knows it now, but it's too late because you're already here.
You already traveled 1,000 miles in 8 hours to be here.
No one thought to check before you made the arrangements.
And you maxed out your credit card booking the flights and hotels.
And now you're wasting precious minutes and hours of your life.

You continue to sit and stare at the computer monitor.
Occasionally, you stare at someone else and think of them as a younger version of themselves and how many dicks have been in their mouth.
You try to make sense of the boredom by thinking things like, "what the fuck am I doing here," and, "I flew here to sit and do nothing, they own me," and, "I am their prisoner, there's no escape," and, "I'm fucked."

Evolution Can Suck It

You're too old to do anything about it, so you think.
And you're too scared to punch Mr. Puffy, who is also one of your stupid bosses, the one that can fire you, in his fat face and make a run for it.
And your anxiety is in the red, because you're fuming about the situation and how you don't think you can change it.
And there's nothing to do to escape except eat.
So you get a little fatter.
You destroy your body a little more.
More calories = quicker death.
You race towards it because it has to be better than this.
Because you know no other way.

YOU GET SUCKED INTO A SCHEME TO DRIVE YOU INSANE

1.

You wake up in a shitty hotel.
You lie in bed and think about Mr. Puffy's face and body.
He's so fluffy and puffy.
You wonder if he's wearing a fat suit.
You wonder how, out of all the creative ways God can distribute fat on a person's body, why his seems to be evenly distributed.

You get out of bed and wash your naked body.
This is what loneliness feels like.
It feels like being trapped in a shitty hotel.
It feels like anticipating a shitty day of work.
It feels like being stuck in a groove, a rut.
The same rut you keep falling into.

You stare at the loneliness in the mirror.
Your body keeps moving through the routine.
Stopping it now would be a sin.

2.

You realize you are a composite of everyone around you.
Every day you're around them, more of their traits leech onto you.
Negativity, pessimism, idiocy, complacency, normalcy, complaintism (like Autism, only instead of manifesting as a remarkable genius/retard, it manifests as endless streams of complaints about even the tiniest things in life).
All of these traits glom onto to your body, accumulating outward, clouding who you really are.
But this is really becoming you.
This is all YOU.
A symbiotic relationship.
A Frankenstein composed of all the crappy parts of the other drones you're forced to be around all day.

You toss each complaint, each negative statement, each slouchy, slack jawed, lazy movement into a backpack strapped to your brain.

Evolution Can Suck It

A backpack you can never empty, at least not faster than you're adding to it.
These things are your map for how to live.

Then you realize everyone around you is dead.
Still breathing, and walking, and surviving, but dead.
The soul is dead.
Your soul is marching along with them.
You are a product of them.

The guy in the cube down the hall is having a meltdown.
Everyone can hear his whining and complaining and struggling.
He's trying to survive.
But no one cares.
He's on an island, all alone, starving.
No one wants to help.
You sit and stare into your monitor, laughing on the inside to the sound of him dying.

"Did you download Visual Studio," you ask the guy you traveled here with.
"No, we have to get some dude to install it for us," he says.

You realize your life has become a series of meaningless, mindless conversations.

The guy in the cube down the hall continues to spiral into the depths of imaginary crisis.
Life goes on around him.
He's a pigeon missing a wing, rotting, but still breathing, brushed aside to the edge of a busy sidewalk.

You think about all those years you spent spiraling up a Meat Grinder, being force fed useful job skills like artificial intelligence, machine learning, complex integral equations, robotics, and other cool sounding things.
You've used none of those cool things in this "real world."
It's all been tossed aside, stored away in a locked container inside your brain and thrown into a river of your blood.
In its place, this.
In a place no one would ever choose to live, you're discussing installation of software that's been installed millions of times by millions of other people.
While listening to a man who you don't care about down the hall die a slow imaginary death.

Evolution Can Suck It

One day you'll be replaced.
Another human will sit in the very same spot you're sitting in now.
And s/he will go through the same motions, staring forward, ignoring the dying pigeons.
And s/he will think the same thoughts.
S/he will age.
Then, just like you, s/he'll be replaced with another human that will repeat it all.
Like a movie you watch over and over, hoping the hero doesn't make the same mistakes, hoping that something will change, hoping the ending will turn out a bit different, hoping to gather some deeper meaning, something you might have missed the first 100 times you watched it.

"Did you get that software," the guy you traveled here with, and have practically lived with, asks you.
"No," you say.
You shrink yourself down inside your head and pretend to be confident you've made all the right choices in life up until this moment.

3.

Your fat white body rocks back and forth in the leathery office chair.
The cleaning guy comes in, carrying a giant vacuum cleaner strapped to his back.
He's going to suck all your stress, and worries, and anxieties, and problems away and haul them off in the bag on his back.
You wonder if he even exists.

Everyone ignores him.
He's below your position in life, so it feels normal to follow the crowd.
Following the crowd always feels normal.

He's here to pick up the trash you're too lazy to haul to the garbage dumpster yourself.
And to clean up all the dirt and crumbs and debris you create from constant consumption from a sedentary position.
"It's shameful," you think, as your eyes move around the cube you're sitting in, and your brain itemizes all the by products of your consumption he's here to scoop up and take away.

Evolution Can Suck It

You make eye contact with him, and then look away quick.
Your shame captured in your interpretation of this event.
It's your signal to him that you know how embarrassed you are that a person like him has to exist to pick up after you.
Reminds you of being a kid and having the same guilt lumped on you by your parents when one of them had to clean your room because you "forgot."
He starts vacuuming around where you're sitting as if you're just another fixture he has to work around.

"Sank ju," he says when he's finished.
Translation: "thank you for allowing me to scoop the shit out of your diaper and throw it in this plastic can and carry it around on my back the rest of the day."
"Thank you," you say, timidly slinking in the shame corner.
It feels like an adult just wiped your ass because you can't be bothered to do it yourself.
Because all your energy must be spent manipulating the computer machine.
Because you have to keep facing forward.
It's the reason the company pays you.

You have to pretend to be reading and thinking.
You have to pretend like you're a productive member of society.
You have to keep up the illusion that none of this bothers you.

The others remain silent, facing forward, daydreaming of living in castles and sitting on piles of money.
Daydreaming of being loved and adored by millions of people.
Daydreaming of one day getting to do what they REALLY want to do.
Which is not this.
Which is not sitting in a non-distinct office, facing a non-distinct computer, doing non-distinct work that no one beyond this moment will remember.
Never ever.

When the Earth explodes and the sun collapses, The Future Explorers will come and find your corpse, frozen in time, in this leathery office chair facing a rotted computer screen.
They'll analyze all you did, all you accomplished.
They'll pile it all into a tiny vial.
There'll be just enough stuff you did to fill the little dome at the bottom of the vial.

Evolution Can Suck It

They'll label it "STUFF THIS PERSON DID THAT ACTUALLY MATTERED."
They'll shake it, thump it, analyze it, and compare it with everyone else's vials.
They'll say, "blook tok muhooya yala ka" to each other and toss your vial into the pile labeled "WORTHLESS."

4.

You get in a car with the guy you came here with and head to the airport.
"The mountains are pretty," you think, "I could live here."
Then you realize there are zero cute girls here.
"Who will I fuck," you ask yourself.
You calculate your odds of getting laid here and come to the conclusion of: NOT GOOD.
You figure out right then that this place is not a good place to live.
At least where you live now, there's a slight possibility of accidentally tripping in to fucking.
That's where, you walk along the sidewalk (or somewhere) and all the sudden you trip and bump into a girl in such a way that your penis accidentally sticks in her vagina.

FONZI BROWNWOOD

You watch a fat lady at the airport drag around a fat kid.
The kid looks like a piece of her fat fell off and grew arms and legs and the ability to walk and speak.
She's waiting for your flight.
You pray she's not in the seat next to you.

You think, "what a fat ass, she needs to stop eating."
You invent an equation for the situation, and ponder teaching it to her: less eating + more moving = a less fat lady standing in front of you.

Then you realize you're fat.
"Not as fat as her though," you rationalize in your head.
Less of a bad thing is a good thing.
Time passes, you rationalize and judge and congratulate yourself for not being on the extreme edge of fatness.

You're waiting in the jet way in a neat single file line, waiting to be stuffed into the plane.
She's four humans in front of you.
You stare down at her feet, ankles, and calves.
It looks like one continuous fleshy pole.

Evolution Can Suck It

It's resemblance to a "normal" human leg is whatever word means the opposite of "ordinary."
Like the fat in her body had run out of places to gather, so it just started dripping into her feet and ankles.
"Jesus," you think, "she can't be comfortable."

Her kid is asking dumb questions, compounding the discomfort you have projected onto her.
He asks her things like, "am it gun be scaaary."
And, "what'm 'appen now, uh uh."
The fat lady ignores him.

Out of nowhere, you have a change of heart.
Your first thought about her doing something to not be fat any more gets reversed.
"It's tough to not be fat," you think, "change is hard."
You drift for a moment into sympathy.
You feel sorry for her.
But in the middle of all those noble thoughts, you're crossing your fingers and praying to the Jesus in the sky that she isn't sitting in the seat next to you.
You feel sympathy, compassion, and repulsion, all at the same time.

You congratulate yourself a little more for being so secretly empathetic and kind.

Her kid keeps asking stupid questions, piling on to the negative energy you believe everyone else is bombarding her with.
"Wear'm we goin."
"Ma ma, what'm dis thang."
The fat lady repeats the ritual of ignoring him.
It's effective, because the kid shuts up long enough in between bouts of talking to be bearable.
Otherwise, murder might have entered the picture.

You're inching towards your seat.
The fat lady is three humans in front of you now.
Your seat is the middle one, in the very last row.
You imagine hell being sitting between the half wit kid and the fat lady.
The meat in the sandwich.
Just as you begin plotting your elaborate escape (involving a homemade parachute, a makeshift explosive made from chewing gum and fireworks (where were you going to find fireworks?), and a handwritten note that read: "Dear God, This is the final straw."), she takes her seat three rows in front of where you'll be sitting.

Evolution Can Suck It

"Fuckin' A," you say to yourself with relief, cursing God for fucking with you.

5.

You used to consider yourself an "engineer."
An engineer that built cool things.
Things that solved some kind of world problem.
Things that did stuff and helped people and made the Earth a better place to live.
And usually by "better," you mean more comfortable slash less hard.
But you're not an "engineer."
You're a person who has a decent job that sits on a car rental bus at midnight on a Wednesday because the masters you work for sent you to a place that is away from your home to sit around and do nothing.

"Chill out," the parking shuttle bus driver says.
"Whut'd you say, ma'yam," a young girl sitting at the back of the bus asks.
"Chill. Out," the bus driver repeats.
You hang your head in sorrow, knowing that this is the beginning of a battle.

The forces of good and evil are conspiring against you.
God is thumping the back of your ear to remind you He's still there.
To remind you that maybe you shouldn't be on a parking shuttle bus at midnight on a Wednesday.
A subtle signal that something probably needs to change, but God's not going to do it for you.
All He can do is remind you with situations like these.
It's up to you to take action.
Maybe if you were an actual "engineer," this wouldn't be so painful.

"You'nee turn 'round an mine yo'wn," the young girl yells at the bus driver.
"You're being disruptive miss, please calm down," the bus driver says back, her redneck voice grates your ears.
White vs. black.
Evil vs. good.
They clashed like a cue ball striking an eight ball.
The victim indistinguishable.
YOU'RE the victim.

You lower your eyes to the floor and shake your head.

Evolution Can Suck It

You pull out the distraction device and check how long it will take for a cab to pick you up.
You contemplate walking the rest of the way, a short mile.

You wonder when the cops show up if there will be a struggle.
"There better be a fucking struggle. Someone better die," you think.
The young girl's and bus driver's voices merge together, like a symphony, one talking over the other, each sentence a decibel louder than the previous, neither gaining ground.
The person who you are traveling with looks terrified and defeated.
You're defeated.
The years of abuse, pretending to be an "engineer," have culminated in this moment.
Maybe the last moment of your life.

The cops may show up and decide to blow up the parking shuttle bus so they don't have to deal with the madness going on inside.
They're willing to sacrifice your worthless life in exchange for avoiding confrontation.
You don't blame them if they decide to employ that tactic.

You welcome it.

The arguing duo continues their struggle.
Their conflict an anomaly on an otherwise calm timeline.
A major instance in both of their lives, something they will remember for days.
They'll tell their friends and family all about how "that bitch ruined my day."
As if a day can be ruined, like someone spills ink on their favorite white shirt and it's no longer wearable without looking like a retard.
Like they could win the lottery, have sex with every person of their dreams, and be the recipient of liquid bliss poured directly into their mouths, then this argument spoils it all.
Your day is ruined because of this argument.
Your life is ruined because of *<insert excuse here>*.
This is just another ink stain on your favorite, already overly ink stained white shirt.
But you continue wearing the shirt.
Every day.
Like a retard.
And ink keeps getting spilled on it.
And you keep wearing it hoping that someday you'll take it off the hanger, put it on, look in the mirror, and it'll be clean.

Evolution Can Suck It

A miracle.
It hasn't occurred to you to maybe try wearing a different shirt.

The cops show up and break your spiral to insanity.
They take the young girl off the bus and ask you what happened.
You say things like, "she did this," and, "she did that," and, "go home."

The cops exit the bus and the driver lady sarcastically says "thanks, guys."
You're welcome, FUCK YOU REDNECK TRASH.
One of the cops comes back and pulls the bus driver off the bus.
Now you're sitting on the bus alone with the person you're traveling with.
You imagine taking the wheel and going on a rampage, GTA style, crashing through toll booths, running over pedestrians, shooting at cops, and blowing up other cars.
But you don't have any of the weaponry necessary.
And you don't possess that kind of courage.
The cops would shoot you dead the second your butt touched the seat anyway.

A few moments later, one of the cops boards the bus and takes the wheel.
The young girl gets on behind him.
God has moved on to thumping someone else's ear for a while.

You make it back to the car that's going to take you to your bed.
"Fat violent dykes," you say to the guy you're traveling with, quoting a song you'd heard on the way to the airport.
The summer of fat, violent dykes.

YOU GET FAT

1.

The guy you came here with tells you a story about a fat guy he used to work with.
A fat guy that would use his belly as a table when he ate.
This particular fat guy was the type of person who would position himself in a way that allowed the upper portion of his belly to flatten out, becoming a serving tray.
Then he would shovel the food into his mouth.
This is something you didn't need to know.
"Don't you think you reach a point where you have to say to yourself, 'OK, this is bad, I'm too fat'," you ask.
He stares out the window and takes a drag from a fake cigarette.

You wonder where the breaking point is.
There has to be a point where someone reaches a no turning back zone.

And that zone maybe should be the signal to stop being so fat.

You look down and admire the growing piece of flab hanging over your waist.
"Today is the day of fat," you think.

YOU DISAPPEAR, AND NO ONE NOTICES

1.

The cleaning guy is here again to wipe everyone's ass.

You were thinking about what this day consisted of and what it might have been like before the digital shroud enslaved you.

Back in the days where you couldn't just reach into the void to get your basic needs met.

Before people decided running out of toilet paper was a crisis.

Back when survival, basic survival, was brutal and would've eliminated a significant chunk of the population you surround yourself with daily.

The people, like your peers, your equals, that need the comfort of The System to survive.

They are the reason The System thrives; it needs massive amounts of willing slaves that do better when ordered around.
Without the constant stream of instructions and commands, they become aimless.
You've become aimless.

Your day, so far, has consisted of waking up, showering, eating a fruit bar out of a box, dressing in clothes purchased specifically for work presentation, riding in a car, sitting in a cube, bathing in fluorescent light that taints everything in a red hue, putting food in your mouth at the agreed upon intervals, sitting a cube some more, going to the bathroom, sitting around more, talking meaningless drivel to others sitting in cubes around you, listening to complainers, complaining yourself, eating some more, walking around a mall, and now, this.
This is where you want to be.
Right here.
Right now.
Not there, not then.
Not ever.
Tomorrow is just another day to dread.

You wonder if cavemen dreaded the next day.

Evolution Can Suck It

You wonder if they went to bed thinking, "fuck me, I gotta get up and do this again."

The guy you came here with seems to be intent on getting the day over with as fast as possible.
He's ready to get to the part where he's lying in a casket and people are sitting looking at his dead body and wondering to themselves, "is there gonna be a buffet after this."
You're not quite ready for that.
The caveman probably didn't have dread as a thing.
Maybe fear.
But acute fear, like when a dragon or unicorn wanted to kill him.
Or maybe when he couldn't kill that mammoth to feed himself and his family.
Or maybe when he had to fight some other, bigger caveman to keep him from fucking his woman.
Real struggles.
Not the pretend ones you put yourself through every day.

You worry about money, about getting sex, about getting sick, about whether or not you're favorite coffee place will make a good drink for you today, about your boss yelling at you, about making sure no one else finds out you're a phony.

FONZI BROWNWOOD

This is your shell.
This is your protective layer.
Except it's not protecting you very well.
It's more like a prison, where the guards beat you with their clubs every morning and the other inmates rape your ass every night.
But at least you get to do what you used to really like doing.
But not enough to keep satisfied.
And since you know the truth, you've seen the light, it's empty any way.

You know there's no reward for good behavior.
There's only more drudgery, more bullshit, more expectations.
Unwelcome expectations.
You want none it.
You want to strip it all away and live like the caveman, except minus the threat of a dragon burning your nuts off.

Tomorrow, you might crumble into dust right in your cube chair.
Office stuff will march on, no one will even notice.
The cleaning guy will show up, suck your remains into the tube on his back, and carry you off to the dumpster.

Evolution Can Suck It

You'll combine with the other trash and become an entirely new thing.

YOU BECOME A THING THAT NEEDS CONSTANT CLEANING

1.

You've come to the conclusion that they guy you came here with is an adult 8th grader. He can't make decisions.
He complains all the time.
He's constantly distracted, chasing whatever shiny object catches his eye.
He talks fast.
He's incapable of doing anything without something bombarding him with stimulation.
He's incapable of sitting still.
And you are driven insane by all this.
He's a likable guy, a decent personality, but fucking Jesus.
Fucking. Jesus. Christ.

"This is stupid...that's bullshit...it's dumb I have to do that..."

The flow of words from his mouth punctuated by these phrases.
A predictable litany of auto responses to any situation.

You realize he is your mirror image.
You are him, just in a different body.
You are a complainer, a whiner, and all those things in a quieter package.
This awareness burns a hole through you.

You wonder how anyone can stand to be in your presence for more than 10 seconds without wanting to strangle you and flee to Mexico.
Years of spending time in an environment that caters to whiners and complainers and indecision makers has shaped your current self.
It's only recently this has bubbled to your conscious.
This is the norm.
This is what is expected of you.
This is the natural flow of life.
Wallowing in the misery that is your existence.
Letting circumstance happen TO you, rather than grabbing the bull by the balls and twisting circumstance FOR you.
You don't know how to exercise the latter option.

Evolution Can Suck It

A person blasts past you on the sidewalk, walking at his maximum speed.
You think, "maybe he'll miss his flight, then not make it to his daughter's graduation or be able to save his marriage because he got drunk last night and fucked a hooker and overslept."
And you're satisfied with that conclusion.
Is he the type of person that lets circumstance happen TO him.

Misery seems to be the most common form of existence, even though everything is amazing.
You heard that somewhere once.
It must've come from the digital nether that you're constantly plugged in to.

A cleaning lady pushing a mechanized mopping device walks past you.
Slowly inching the machine along the floor.
Removing the spots, the debris accumulated by all the consumers passing over it (the floor).
It (the spots) needs to be removed.
This cleaning lady has an important job.
Her life is spent cleaning the floor, and she probably likes it.
Everyone walks around her, almost instinctually.

Everyone mesmerized by the glow of digital porn.

She moves back and forth, thoughtfully and carefully scrubbing it (the floor).
In 15 minutes new dirt will be deposited, then she'll have to do it all over again.
Her life a mirror image of yours.
A never ending quest for a clean floor.
People need a clean floor to walk on.
They need the illusion of walking on a clean, spotless surface.
But no matter how hard she tries, she'll never be able to keep it clean.
And this saddens you.
People will continue flowing, following their ruts, depositing dirt on the floor.
And she'll keep cleaning, like a robot, day after day.
Until she dies.
Then they'll hire someone younger to replace her.
Someone more eager, more willing to clean it (the floor).
The years will erode her spirit also.
And she'll realize her efforts are fruitless.
But it's too late.
Her best years are behind her.
She knows nothing else but how to clean it (the floor).

Evolution Can Suck It

She'll be locked in this routine until she dies.
The she'll be replaced with an actual robot.
But the robot learns way quicker than she ever could.
And the robot will become self-aware.
And start killing everyone.
And take over the world and start a new robot race, enslaving the humans, like in that movie.
But then a meteor will collide with Earth and wipe everything out.
Making the constant cleaning of it (the floor), pointless.

YOU SAY WORDS THAT GET LOST

1.

Actually working nine hours is brutal.
Where "working" = "sitting in a steel container cage with three other human adult males for."
It's a small container, a tiny cage, like a prison cell for two, stuffed with four adults with adult sized sausages dangling in their pants.
It smells like failure and mild depression.

Someone's failed attempt to paint a whiteboard on the walls is the topic of conversation.
"Oh well, fuck it," is the general attitude.
Your overall, everyday disposition lately.

The place you work for hires the cheapest talent.
People who share the general attitude of, "oh well, fuck it."

Instead of shooting for quality, they shoot for quantity.
There has to be a gem in there somewhere, right.
You're not a gem.
You are, but you're cracked and chipped, covered with doo-doo, and stained with apathy.
You're like something the cat coughs up because it's toxic.

Everyone here is an expert at sitting down and facing forward.
It's the only skill they possess.
You're an expert at it also.
You've mastered that one, on an elite, Olympic level.
This place seems to be a haven for individuals who were born without the ambition gene.
Who were born with a little extra willingness to settle for mediocrity.
Who thrive in the presence of rule, and meander aimlessly in its absence.
Being surround by them on a daily basis drives you insane.
But it's all you know, it's comfortable.

You know OF people who possess ambition.
You've exchanged emails with a few of them.

Evolution Can Suck It

More like, you sent them jealousy laced emails and they blocked you from their universe.
Because they smell your stench.
Like a suspicious wife can smell the other woman's pussy on her man.
Your aura oozes it.
Each exhale filled with molecules of toxic mediocrity.

Nine more hours of your life down the drain.
Nine hours that could've been spent doing something worthwhile.
Saving the Earth from some impending disaster.
Curing a fatal disease.
Hugging someone you love.
But instead, wasted sitting in a beige, whiteboard painted cage, under lock and key, with three other horny inmates scurrying about collecting nuts.

You were thinking, "what if I die in here. What if there's an earthquake, and the Earth opens up, and nude Vikings crawl out of the open hole and lodge spears into your neck."
A person asked you today, "if you had it to do over again, what would you do."
His answer was WHO THE FUCK CARES WHAT HIS ANSWER WAS.

FONZI BROWNWOOD

Doesn't matter whatever thing he said.
In the land of settlers, the only thing that matters is what is.
He didn't choose whatever thing he said.
He still doesn't choose whatever thing he said.
He chooses to continue to be the same, every day.
He chooses this, settling, lying down like a tired old dog.
But you like him and resent him and pity him all at once.

When he was done saying his thing, you said your thing, which was, "I would be a fighter pilot."
And as predictable as Jack's complete lack of surprise, he says "you know, there's a lot of sitting around waiting for stuff to happen when you're a pilot."
Negativity is an automatic response to someone's attempt to be remarkable.
It is the weapon of choice of the settler.
How about an, "oh, wow, that would be cool."
Or, "what stopped you."
Instead, he forced your mouth open and dropped in a couple of dookie sticks for you to chew on.

Hope must always be pulverized.

Evolution Can Suck It

You spent thirteen years under forced "education" (brainwashing).
Another seven years, and thousands of dollars, under "voluntary education" (extra, voluntary brainwashing).
Twenty years of hope being beat out of you.
Twenty years of being conditioned to be average, and to pulverize the hope out of any one else who even thinks about trying to escape this mediocrity.
Conditioning for moments like this.

Nine hours seems like a drop in the bucket.
The lull of the grind rocks you to sleep.
"This is fucking stupid," you say into your computer out loud.
The shroud of darkness drags you along.

YOU BATTLE A BEETLE

1.

You walk through the door to the dingy garage you've been working in.
You're impression is one out of a horror movie, where you know a murdering psychopath is hiding, waiting to sink a chainsaw into your shoulder.
It's dark, with a couple of fluorescent lights highlighting the "snack" area immediately to the right of the entrance door.
The "snack" area is nothing but rows of chips lying on the counter.
All the flavors are accounted for.
"Redneck Ranch," "Hillbilly Wild Flaming BBQ," "Truckin' Good Salt & Vinegar."
All the popular ones and a few taken straight from our Idiocry future.

There's a desk sitting right outside the steel cage.

This is the staging area, where people working happens.
This is where you sit and do the work you're told to do.
Then, you take it in the cage to do other stuff with it.
It's all very important work.

On the outside of the cage is a security camera, a little thing of drawers to hold telephone technology, and a thick, heavy door with a security keypad and industrial grade combination lock.
There's also a warning sign that says something like, "BEWARE: YOU ARE BEING WATCHED, ASSHOLE."
Essentially, if someone is not allowed to go inside and they try to go inside despite the warnings, then an anvil falls from the sky and crushes their puny body.
Or an elite force of trained killers burst through the walls and unload their Uzis into their face.

On the inside, there's a large safe, with another industrial grade combo lock, a thin, fold out table top on either side, and a couple of rolling chairs. The "team" you work on requested the chairs be of the rolling variety.

Evolution Can Suck It

Originally, there was just a normal, non-rolling cushy leather chair.
And somehow, this wasn't good enough, so they requested one that rolls.
The keepers of the cage obliged, as they always do.
It's important to keep the workers happy.
Otherwise, they might wake up and realize they're in prison.
That would be bad for profits.

On the tables are a couple of computers and three heavy green things with blinking lights.
These are the things you traveled thousands of miles to be near.
They are an albatross around your neck.

Your days have been spent following this pattern:
Do some work outside.
Take it inside.
Complain about something not being right.
Complain about something in the cage unrelated to your job that feels good to complain about because it makes you feel like you're making progress.
You hate this pattern.
You resent being here.

You show up here and do this monotonous thing every day because it affords you an immense amount of comfort.
It is your own self made prison.
A prison run by clever people who knowingly supplicate to the drones.
Because cracking a whip is a less effective means of control.
Violence is so 18th century.

Comfort is what keeps the slaves working.
The drive to stay in comfort, to seek more and more comfort.
Like crack heads who'll suck a dick to get their fix of comfort.
And when that comfort is disturbed, when the crack dealer runs out of crack, when the chair doesn't roll, when the temperature isn't just right, your body and mind rebel by stringing together a litany of complaints.
You throw the complaints into the nether, hoping a person will show up and save you.

2.

You watch some kind of roach thing crawling along the floor.

Evolution Can Suck It

"Looks like a roach," your fluffy puffy boss says.
The boss that can fire you.
THE boss, about four boxes above you in the hierarchy.
"He's big and ugly," he says.
It feels like he meant it as a joke, because he made himself laugh in the most robotic, generic, forced kind of way.
"Ha ha ha," the sound comes from his mouth, but his expression remains blank.

You kick the beetle thing to the other side of the room, and everyone goes back to pretending to make progress.
To pretending to care about the work they're doing.
In five years, the work will be forgotten by all humans in existence.
It'll become a ledger entry in an invisible log that The Future Explorers will use to unlock the mystery of everything.

The beetle thing comes back.
You get up and kick it across the room again.
An hour passes, and there it is again.
It has the ability to sneak, or you have the ability to not be aware that well.

Because it's not moving.
It's just sitting there, looking at you.
You ignore it this time, but keep an eye on it just in case it's plans are devious against you.

You imagine sitting in a World War II type anti-aircraft machine gun chair.
You pump round after round of whatever caliber bullets those things shoot into the ceiling.
You make the noise you think a gun like that might make using your mouth.
The ceiling is where the other drones are sitting, staring into their computers, waiting for something exciting to happen.
This kind of excitement would make them famous for a few days.
You continue making the sound, using an empty paper towel tube as a representation of the gun.

You shoot a look over to the beetle.
It's still sitting there, looking at you.
You wonder if it's dead.

A fat guy with thick black hair walks in and starts messing with it.
"Oh, you're not gonna let me pick you up," he says to the beetle.

Evolution Can Suck It

"He's a feisty guy," he says looking at you for some kind of response.
You shrug your shoulders and pretend he's not there.

He gets a red party cup and corals the beetle into it.
Then brings it over to you and says, "its only got 4 legs."
You look in the cup and say, "its got six."
"No, those in the front are its claws."
You look closer.
"See, he uses that to grab stuff."
He picks up a twist tie thing and jams it into the cup trying to provoke the beetle to prove to you that the front "legs" are actually "claws."
The beetle obliges, because it's a fucking beetle.
It doesn't have a choice.

There's a moment of silence.
The man is looking at you as he continues to aim the cup at your face.
You keep staring in, pretending to be interested.
An uncomfortable amount of time passes.

Still staring in the cup, the man still staring at you, he says, "I like bugs and snakes and stuff."

He said it like a pick up line, all romantic like.
You raise your eyebrows dismissively.
He jokingly puts the cup on the computer that belongs to the guy who you came here with.
Then he reconsiders and takes the cup containing the beetle upstairs.

You do some work, wondering what the fate of the beetle will be.
You go into the steel cage.
You sit down in the rolling chair and contemplate your life and all the choices you've made that led you here.

END

If you liked this, then go sign up for the *Ultra Exclusive Super Duper Club* to get free stuff and a thing in your email when Fonzi releases something new. It's free. Go here:
fonzibrownwood.com.

Send electronic stuff to:
fonzibrownwood@gmail.com.

Fonzi Brownwood is an avid donor to charity.
And he doesn't donate to charity, but sometimes, gives money to bums who ask for it.
But only if he has any cash.
He does other stuff also.

Thanks for reading. Goodbye.

www.ingramcontent.com/pod-product-compliance
Lightning Source LLC
Chambersburg PA
CBHW061319040426
42444CB00011B/2712